The
GAME
INVENTOR'S
GUIDEBOOK

Brian Tinsman

Published By

kp **krause publications**
An F&W Publications Company

700 East State Street • Iola, WI 54990-0001
715-445-2214 • 888-457-2873
www.krause.com

Please call or write for our free catalog of publications. Our toll-free number to place or obtain a free catalog is (800) 258-0929.
Library of Congress: 2002117372
ISBN: 0-87349-552-7

Cover Images: **Game boxes from Monopoly, The Settlers of Catan, Who Wants To Be A Millionaire, Uno, Trivial Pursuit, Axis & Allies, Pokémon Trading Card Game, and Magic: the Gathering. Rulebooks from the Star Wars Roleplaying Game and Dungeons & Dragons.**

Foreword

This book is really just for one person, but I'm not sure who it is yet.

In 1984 *Trivial Pursuit* shocked the industry by selling 20 million copies and defining the new category of adult party games. *Dungeons & Dragons* started the fantasy roleplaying game category with its breakout success in 1980. In 1993 *Magic: the Gathering* created a category called trading card games, destroying all sales records and becoming one of the best-selling games in the world in a few short years. Today the game world is due for the next category-defining blockbuster product. The idea is probably out there right now. If you're the lucky person destined to create it, this book is for you. I hope I can be part of it by helping you understand what challenges you'll face.

But even if you're not that person, if you have an interesting idea for a game and a lot of perseverance, you have a good shot at getting published. Every year game companies release more than 400 new game products, many of them staggeringly mediocre. There's demand for good ideas. The game industry is one of the few remaining fields where you can have a brainstorm and have a good chance of seeing it on a store shelf within a year. Few other endeavors reward original thinking so well.

I talk to many, many inventors who have a game idea and aren't sure what to do with it. For years I played or reviewed about 150 games a year in every imaginable stage of completion. I was the guy you wanted to impress when your game arrived on my desk. You might be surprised to learn that I've often found myself on the other side of that desk as well. I've had the experience of trying to sell games to publishers and I know how difficult it is to get started. I hope that hearing the advice and stories of those who have been successful will help you get your bearings and perhaps even help you forge your own path through the untamed wilderness of game inventing.

Acknowledgments

I'd like to thank the following individuals for their invaluable help. Alan Moon, Alex Tinsman, Brian Brogaard, Brian Hersch, Frank DiLorenzo, Gary Gygax, Jeff Grubb, Jill Waller, Jonathan Tweet, Jordan Weisman, Joyce Greenholdt, Karen O'Brien, Kristin Looney, Lou Zocchi, Mark Osterhaus, Mike Fitzgerald, Mike Gray, Mike Selinker, Paul Randles, Peggy Brown, Peter Adkison, Reiner Knizia, Richard Garfield, Richard Tait, Robert Gutschera, Ryan Miller, Shawn Williams, Steve Peek, W. Craig Gaines, Whit Alexander, William Murray.

Contents

4

About the Author

Brian Tinsman grew up near Sacramento, California, graduated from the University of California, Berkeley, and earned an MBA from the University of Washington in Seattle. He started his career in the game business as a market research manager, conducting more than 200 hours of consumer testing, watching kids try to learn the rules to games like *Pokémon* and *Magic* through a one-way mirror. This experience was invaluable in helping him understand the needs of game consumers. A lifelong gamer, he has designed or contributed to over twenty published game products, with more on the way. Some of his notable titles Include *Magic: the Gathering Judgment*, *Pokémon Thunderstorm*, and the party game of *Curses*, which won the 2002 MENSA Select award.

Today, Brian is a professional game designer for Wizards of the Coast. He is also the company's concept acquisition lead, reviewing new games from professional inventors. Brian lives near Seattle, Washington with his wife Alex, daughter Phoenix, and mastiff Draco. He's always interested in hearing opinions about games, new ideas, and feedback on this book. Brian's Web site is a resource for people interested about the game industry. It contains information for inventors looking for help with their game ideas. You can contact Brian via his Web site or at:

Brian Tinsman

P.O. Box 1294
Renton, WA 98057

www.briantinsman.com

SECTION ONE

HOW THEY DID IT

Pikachu   50 HP ⚡
                              Basic Pokémon

Mouse Pokémon. Length: 1' 4", Weight: 13 lbs.

⭐ **Quick Attack** Flip a coin. If heads, this
    attack does 10 damage plus 20 more damage;   **10+**
    if tails, this attack does 10 damage.

⚡⚡ **Agility** Flip a coin. If heads, during your
⭐   opponent's next turn, prevent all effects of   **20**
    attacks, including damage, done to Pikachu.

weakness   resistance   retreat cost

*It raises its tail to check its surroundings. The tail is
sometimes struck by lightning in this pose.*   LV. 15   #25

Illus. Naoye Kimura   ©1995–2000 Nintendo, Creatures, GAMEFREAK.   70/111 ●

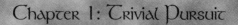

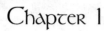

Chapter 1

Trivial Pursuit

Chris Haney and Scott Abbott

The story of *Trivial Pursuit* is a lesson in perseverance. In 1979, Chris Haney was a young photo editor in Montreal and his friend Scott Abbott was a sportswriter with the Canadian Press. Chris, known for having an offbeat sense of humor, and Scott, known for his near-photographic memory, sat down to play *Scrabble* one afternoon and discovered some pieces were missing. Wishing for something new anyway, the pair wondered aloud why they shouldn't invent a game of their own. Why not indeed? They created the basic concept of *Trivial Pursuit* that afternoon. After taking on Chris' brother John and his friend Ed Werner as partners and two years of intense development and fund-raising, the first 1,100 *Trivial Pursuit* sets were printed and ready to sell in 1981.

Inexperienced as they were, expenses turned out to be higher than they expected—a lot higher. All told, those first 1,100 games cost around $82,000 to produce. That's almost $75 apiece! Approaching individual stores in person, they managed to sell all 1,100 games to retailers for $15 each, for a crushing financial loss of close to $65,500.

Over 60 grand in the red, most of us would have cut our losses and given up at this point, but Chris and Scott still believed in their original vision. They resolved to press forward. The Montreal and New York Toy Fairs of 1982 brought more bad news when they booked fewer than 400 orders and two major publishers evaluated the game and rejected it. At that point Chris had spent his life's savings and had sold nearly everything he owned to keep the business alive. All might have been lost save for the fact that some Canadian stores had sold out of their initial orders and were beginning to ask for more. Desperate for money and already deep in debt, they managed to take a $75,000 loan against personal liability and printed another 20,000 games. Though they still struggled with outrageous manufacturing costs, they sold all 20,000 and just managed to break even. At this point the publisher Selchow & Righter took notice, and the inventors soon had a licensing contract in hand.

Still operating on an emaciated marketing budget, they hit on a novel promotional tactic. They sent the game to celebrities whose names appeared in the questions, along with a note saying, "Did you know you're in this game?" Many of the celebrities loved it, and as these high-profile actors and sports stars began to evangelize the game, newspaper and magazine coverage generated tremendous free publicity.

Within a year, sales skyrocketed like never before in game history. They sold over 3 million games in 1983, and over 20 million in 1984, making it the fastest-selling board game in history. Hasbro picked up *Trivial Pursuit* in 1991 and it's now published in 17 languages, with new editions released regularly. Chris and Scott retired as multimillionaires.

Part of Chris and Scott's real genius was their vision of a game aimed at adults; one that adults would be willing to buy for $29.95 a box, which was considered an outrageous price at the time. Until then, there were essentially no games priced above $20 in the stores. Conventional wisdom dictated that games were mostly for kids, and parents weren't willing to spend that much for a game their kid might only play a few times. Chris and Scott's willingness to risk everything they owned shooting for an untapped market resulted in the creation of an entirely new category of adult board games.

Trivial Pursuit
Genus 5

Chapter 2

Magic: the Gathering

Dr. Richard Garfield

Richard Garfield is possibly the most successful game designer in the world and his story is among the most incredible in all of gaming history. His 1990 brainstorm created a new game category that grew into a billion-dollar industry only nine years later.

An unassuming man with a wry sense of humor, Richard grew up in Nepal, Bangladesh, Massachusetts, and Oregon. He went to college at The University of Pennsylvania for both his undergraduate degree and his doctorate degree in combinatorial mathematics. Growing up, games were a big part of Richard's life. Richard recalls, "My junior high school emphasized learning to enjoy learning. While I was there I put together a class in which students could show up and play games. I began to

Richard Garfield

understand there was no part of gaming that was out of bounds for education. After attending, then teaching many more years of school, I believe this just as strongly. All my experience supports the idea that lessons learned in games have a greater impact than lessons learned any other way—short of actual experience."

The first game Richard tried to get published was called *Robo Rally*, a board game in which players use cards to plan out moves several turns in advance. With no game industry experience, he and his friend Mike Davis set out to find an interested publisher. The first one they approached gave a curt

Magic cards

"no thanks," as did the second, and the fifth, and the tenth. Over the course of the next seven years they solicited countless publishers with the game, and met a brick wall each time. To make matters worse, the larger publishers made it clear that he should leave game design to the experts if he couldn't see all the flaws in his design the way they could.

It was this attitude that drew Richard to a smaller, more open-minded company called Wizards of the Coast. In fact, Wizards was really a one-man operation. Peter Adkison, an engineer for Boeing, had recently founded Wizards and ran it out of his basement to publish role-playing game supplements he and his friends had written. Richard recalls, "Wizards appealed to me because Peter seemed like he sincerely wanted to publish new games and wasn't averse to trying new ideas." It was clear that they were both in the business because they loved games, not for the money. Richard pitched *Robo Rally* to Peter in 1990 and to his complete lack of surprise, was turned down yet again. Board games were expensive to produce, Peter explained, and it would be tough to cover expenses since such a small company couldn't generate big orders. However, Peter mentioned he would be interested if Richard could invent a game that was portable and played quickly. Richard had never had a request before, so he readily took the challenge.

For years, Richard had been playing around with ideas for a game that was "bigger than what came in the box." Drawing inspiration from a classic science-fiction strategy game called *Cosmic Encounter*, he envisioned a game that set up rules, then let every card in the game break them in different ways. Further, no player

11

would really know all the powers every card might have—players would constantly be surprised. Only genius could bridge the gap between imagining such a game and actually designing it. "I had no idea if such a game could be designed," Richard recalls, "But I decided to give it a shot."

His "shot" was heard 'round the gaming world. He presented Peter with *Magic: the Gathering*, a fantasy-themed card game where players assume the roles of dueling wizards, summoning creatures and casting spells with which to do battle. The game came in both decks and in 15-card packs with different levels of rarity, much the way baseball trading cards are sold. Good players not only had to play the game well, they also had to constantly search out and trade for the different cards they wanted.

Richard and Peter knew right away that they had something big. Early Wizards employee Lisa Stevens recalls, "I thought the game might make a million, even two or three million dollars!" She was off by a factor of about 300. The first printing of 2.5 million cards was scheduled to last from August through the end of the year. The entire print run sold out the weekend of the game's release at the 1993 Gen Con game convention. Trading card games became an overnight phenomenon that surpassed even *Trivial Pursuit* at its height. Today,

Trading card games

Magic is still the most widely played trading card game with a base of over seven million players in 52 countries. At the time of this writing, it was selling over $100 million a year worldwide, with sales still increasing.

During the several years following *Magic's* release, scores of companies tried to duplicate its success. A few trading card games rose to the top and the rest failed. Later games such as *Pokémon* and *Yu-Gi-Oh* found tremendous success, with *Pokémon* even surpassing *Magic* sales. Richard and Wizards had created a new game category that outsold all other hobby game categories combined.

During his tenure as Wizards of the Coast Game Designer-In-Chief, Richard designed many more successful games, even getting *Robo Rally* published in 1995. Richard owned a significant percentage of Wizards of the Coast when Hasbro bought the company for more than $325 million in 1998. Today, he's still heavily involved in the industry, working on ideas that push the boundaries and question the assumptions of accepted game principles.

A friendly game of Magic: the Gathering

Chapter 3

Dungeons & Dragons

Gary Gygax and Dave Arneson

G ary Gygax and Dave Arneson are universally regarded as the revolutionaries who created the role-playing games industry with their release of *Dungeons & Dragons*. *D&D* has inspired hundreds of imitators, influenced nearly all fantasy games (especially in the computer gaming world), and continues to dominate the industry today, selling in excess of $15 million a year.

In 1969 Gary was an underwriter for an insurance company in Lake Geneva, Wisconsin. At the time, his main passion was playing tactical wargames with about 20 friends who would meet regularly at Gary's house. Tactical wargames are simulations of historical battles using miniature figurines (toy soldiers) on a huge tabletop covered with tiny hills, trees, and assorted terrain. These games

Gary Gygax

required an enormous amount of rules detail to simulate the historical battle conditions as accurately as possible. Players used tape measures to mark exactly how far each figure could move and shoot, based on real-world statistics, with a single game potentially

14

Dave Arneson

lasting all day. That year Gary and his friend Jeff Perren wrote up a version of the rules they had devised, calling the booklet "*Chainmail.*"

A couple of years later Gary met Dave Arneson at the fourth annual Gen Con game convention. Dave had used wargaming rules to create a fantasy battle in which adventurers had to sneak through castle sewers. Instead of finding human guards, the players were surprised by a dragon made from a toy brontosaurus with a clay head. Gary was excited by the idea of fantasy scenarios and the two of them agreed to collaborate on a new set of rules for adventures with wizards, monsters, and magic. Gary also obtained an educational supply catalog and ordered several sets of "platonic solids," soon to be known as four, six, eight, ten, twelve, and twenty-sided dice. They finished "*The Fantasy Game*" quickly and tried to sell it to a number of publishers, but it was immediately rejected. Gary quit his day job in 1973 to commit himself to game design full time. He made a little money repairing shoes in his basement during these lean months. About this time, Gary and Dave formed a publishing company they called TSR, short for "Tactical Studies Rules."

Everyone seemed to agree "*The Fantasy Game*" was an awful title. In January of 1974, Gary drew up what he calls a "Chinese menu" of names, and asked people to pick one item from column A and one item from column B. (Those who have played the earliest versions of *D&D* will no doubt recognize Gary's minor obsession with charts.) Contending names included "Swords & Spells" and "Magic & Monsters," but it was a 5-year-old, Gary's youngest daughter, whose vote tipped the scales for the name "*Dungeons & Dragons.*"

Another partner, Brian Blume, financed the printing, and by October 1974 they had sold 1,000 copies, all through word-of-mouth. In November they ran another 2,000 copies, which sold out in 5 months. Soon they had over 1,000 copies a month going out the door, a remarkable achievement for a product with virtually no marketing. Gary points out "The entire growth of *D&D* was all market pull—no push. We had customers begging retailers to carry it, and the retailers calling us up to order it." Such a situation was almost unbelievable for a small group of gamers who had just started out having fun with their hobby. Sales continued to double every six months.

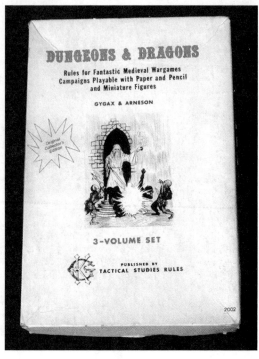

In 1978, TSR released a new version of the game, *Advanced Dungeons & Dragons*. It was a comprehensive, more versatile game than the original, but some saw it as an attempt to cut Dave Arneson out of the business and deny him royalties by changing the game's title. In fact, Dave later won a court judgment against TSR based on this argument.

D&D 3-Volume Box Set

A year later, James Dallas Egbert III, a Michigan college student, suddenly disappeared. A detective on the case speculated that Egbert had tried to experience a *D&D* adventure by exploring the tunnels underneath the campus, perhaps being killed by blasts of steam. Egbert showed up soon after—he had actually gone to visit a friend without telling his parents—but his return didn't get the same media coverage as his disappearance. The story generated unexpected nationwide publicity, and *D&D* sales quadrupled that year. By 1982, sales had broken $20 million.

Though TSR went through some tremendous ups and downs, eventually being purchased by Wizards of the Coast, *D&D* is currently healthier than ever and available in almost every game and large bookstore in the U.S. and Europe.

Chapter 4

The Pokémon Trading Card Game

Tsunekaz Ishihara, Kouichi Ooyama, Takumi Akabane

The *Pokémon Trading Card Game* was released in October of 1996 and in less than five years became the best-selling game of all time. If you didn't blink your eyes and read that last sentence again, you should. In less than five years, the *Pokémon TCG* sold more than *Monopoly* did over 65 years or *Trivial Pursuit* did over 18 years. That's 13 billion cards and more than $3 billion.

Intellectual Property, (abbreviated IP) is industry-speak for the characters and story in a game, TV show, book, or other storytelling medium. *Pokémon's* IP is widely regarded as the most successful kid's property ever. At the height of its popularity you could buy *Pokémon* underwear, toothbrushes, and breakfast cereal, but nothing came close to the sales numbers the card game produced.

The world of *Pokémon* (short for Pocket Monsters) details the adventures of Ash, a boy who's trying to capture and train enough of these strange creatures to become a master. In this world, kids who want to become *Pokémon* masters wander the countryside capturing wild Pokémon in mystic capsules called Pokéballs, training and then battling them against each other in special stadiums. To an adult, there's a lot of really weird stuff going on that doesn't seem to make much sense, but that's actually part of the appeal. The real world doesn't make much sense to a kid either, so when trying to understand the land of *Pokémon*, adults are confused while kids are in their element.

The idea for *Pokémon* started with Gamefreak, a software development group looking for a new way to use the Nintendo Game Boy handheld electronic game unit. Nintendo had recently developed cables that allowed players to link up two Game Boy units and exchange information. Satoshi Tajirii, a 25-year-old software game designer invented the idea for the Game Boy version of *Pokémon* in 1990 and brought it to Nintendo, who decided to publish it. It was a role-playing game based on collecting and exchanging items and monsters. Along the way Tajiri, Tsunekazu Ishihara, and Takashi Kawaguchi created the most important element of the game—a story about a boy who goes on an adventure, catches and exchanges Pokémon, and grows up.

It took six years to develop the Game Boy version. Plagued by shortages of funds, the game turned out to be more complex than Gamefreak expected. They also had to deal with changing cartridge specifications, which again ate up more money, manpower, and time. The Game Boy verson was finally released, and as it gained popularity, Ishihara, one of the original Game Boy *Pokémon* designers, along with card game designers Kouichi Ooyama and Takumi Akabane invented the trading card game. Mr. Akabane recalled, "When we looked at the Game Boy *Pokémon* game, we saw that the characters, interactions, and everything going on with the

Pokémon box set & single booster packs

game were a perfect match for a trading card game. It was a natural fit."

Wizards of the Coast received the license to produce the cards in the U.S. It's hard to appreciate the explosive magnitude of demand for *Pokémon* cards when the American version of the TV show was released in 1998. Wizards had the power of life and death over many retail businesses as they chose which orders to fill first. "At that point, it was like we were just printing money," says *Pokémon* developer Mike Elliott. There actually weren't enough printing presses in the country to meet the demand for *Pokémon* cards. In fact, a number of sports card series were discontinued in 1999 solely because the sports card companies couldn't find anyone to print them—every available printer was churning out *Pokémon* cards as fast as possible.

Sales were strong enough that Wizards used some of the profits to open a chain of their own retail outlets in malls throughout America. Since the Wizards stores always had their product orders filled first, they were often the only place *Pokémon* cards were available. Demand was so high that game store owners whose orders hadn't been filled came to the Wizards stores, purchased huge amounts at full retail price ($9.95 per deck), brought them back to their own stores, and marked them up at double the retail price ($19.95 per deck). Even at that price they sold out immediately. Wizards felt this practice was unfair to the kids who stood in line for hours only to have a shopkeeper buy up all the product in the store. Wizards managers started limiting purchases to one deck per customer.

In defiance of this rule, one competing store owner actually rented a bus, went to a shelter, and filled up the bus with transients. He brought all of them to the store, gave each one $10, and had each transient buy a deck for him. He drove them around to every Wizards store in the area before the day was through.

So what was it about this game that made kids so crazy to buy it? I spoke with Robert Gutschera, the game development lead for the *Pokémon TCG's* American release.

Brian: "Why do you think the *Pokémon Trading Card Game* is so successful?"

Robert: "There are a few reasons I can think of. First, the TV show came out and was incredibly popular right away. No one had expected it to be that big, so basically the *Pokémon TCG* happened to be the only good merchandise available at the time. In fact, the next best option for a collector at the time was to get the *Pokémon* plush dolls from a promotion at KFC, of which there were only four available. Apart from that, the card game was your only choice for collecting. But even after more merchandise came out, the game was a lot better than anything else you could buy.

"Look at the world of *Pokémon*. *Pokémon's* big thing is 'Gotta catch 'em all.' Well, 'all' is a lot. There are 150 Pokémon, so what kind of product can you buy to get all of them? You could buy some figurines, but nobody made 150 different ones. With the card game you could be sure of getting every last Pokémon, plus the game had the best artwork and all the statistics so you could learn all about them too.

"Of course, when it really started to take off, it just gained momentum. When you see other kids playing them at school, you want to have some yourself, and so it sort of markets itself. The show itself is all about competition and the game really lets you experience that as well."

Brian: "So a big part of the game's popularity comes from the characters and story. What made the story so successful?"

Robert: "The experience of being a kid is that you feel like you have no power. You want a candy bar, mom won't let you. You don't want to go to bed, but you have to anyway. Now look at the world of *Pokémon*. The main characters are basically on their own wandering around with nobody to tell them what to do. That's pretty cool for a kid. Their goal is to go out and find monsters and capture them. Now normally monsters are scary, but *Pokémon* monsters are kind of cute, even though they're powerful. You, the kid, control the monsters. Something that maybe used to scare you (think monsters under the bed) now is something you control, something that obeys your commands. That's pretty cool. And the main character, Ash, just wanders around with his buddies trying to challenge other kids and gain respect. How cool is that? Kids really identify with it.

19

"Kids like to collect things and they like to master knowledge. Look at kids who know all the names of various dinosaurs. If you're a kid it's pretty powerful to know something your parents don't even know. Now *Pokémon* comes along and there's a ton of information you can learn about. You can learn their names, their powers, how they evolve, it's a lot of information, but not too much. Now you can know a lot of things that your friends and parents don't and that's cool for a kid."

Those who understand the industry say that once a phenomenon becomes popular enough, it acts as "social currency." If you want to talk to film buffs, you need to know *The Godfather* and *Citizen Kane*. If you wanted to be accepted in any social group of American kids in 1999 and 2000, you had to know about *Pokémon*.

The game is still a strong seller both in Japan and the U.S., though it's nowhere near the levels of its peak years. To the chagrin of the doomsayers who thought it would be a flash in the pan, *Pokémon* looks like it actually has some staying power.

Pokémon cards

Chapter 5

Interview With an Inventor

Dr. Reiner Knizia

Reiner Knizia

Reiner Knizia is among the most respected game designers in the industry. With over 100 published titles and dozens and dozens of awards, he is not only one of the most talented, but possibly the most prolific inventor in the world. His games have sold a combined total of several million copies. Some of his recent notable games include *Lord of the Rings* (Games 100 Best Family Strategy Game, 2002), *Lost Cities* (Gamer's Choice Award, 2000), and *Quandary* (Games 100 Best Family Strategy Game 1998).

A native of Germany, Reiner recalls in an interview on the Web site www.discovergames.com, "I have been designing games for as long as I can remember. ...at the age of about ten I used to see games in shop windows, but could not afford to buy them. Instead I decided

21

to make my own." Through trial and error, Reiner began to learn the basics of what made good and bad games. "Later, when able to afford to buy the games, I found that the ones I wanted did not exist, and so continued to design my own."

After earning a doctorate in mathematics he found a career at a large bank in Munich. During these years Reiner would get up at about 5:30 a.m. and work on game designs in the quiet hours of the morning before leaving for work. This time, combined with every other spare moment he could find, gave him about twenty hours a week to work on designs.

Though he had already published a book of games and written many games for periodicals, he sold his first boxed games to

Knizia's Tutanchamun

German companies Hexagames and Hans im Gluck in 1991. From there, he steadily sold more games each year until he finally decided to quit his day job and pursue games full time. Early in his career he focused mainly on the German game market, but today his games are just as likely to end up with an American company as any other. For example, in 2001 he had new games published by twenty different companies throughout North America and Europe! I met Reiner at the Origins game convention in Columbus, Ohio in July of 2002. A friendly, well-spoken man, one only has to meet him to sense how much he loves his work.

Brian: "How did you sell your first game?"

Reiner: "It was pretty straightforward. I contacted the publisher and showed them the games and they liked them. Remember I had been designing games on my own for twenty years before then."

Brian: "Where do you start when inventing a new game?"

Reiner: "Well, you can't always start at the same corner, or you'll always end up in the same corner. That's the problem with game design—there is no consistent approach. Taking the same approach goes against creativity. Game design really is an art, not a science. You can't apply the same methodology or you'll come up with the same type of game."

Brian: "What do you do if you have trouble selling a certain game?"

22

Reiner: "If the publishers don't like it I rework it. I have only a handful of games that haven't sold, and for those I feel probably it's the right thing they aren't published. Publishers are a good second opinion on how good a game is, and I really wouldn't want my name on a game that's not very good. I'm a perfectionist and I stand behind all the games I have published."

Brian: "What are some of the problems you've had to overcome in inventing new games?"

Reiner: "My biggest problem is that I am unable to clone myself [laughing]. I have so many ideas. There are so many projects I could do, but there isn't enough time in the week to do them all. It's difficult to choose which ones to work on first. People start stealing my ideas before I even have them! This isn't paranoia—just an extreme sense of urgency."

Brian: "What's an important lesson you've learned about game inventing?"

Reiner: "Different people expect different things from games. You need to know the audience you're creating the game for. Do they want an easy game with very fast rules for the mass market or a deep strategic game for experienced game players? It's important to remember that in the end all that counts is the quality of the game. But the quality criteria change—they are defined by the market."

Brian: "Where would you recommend a new inventor start when creating a game?"

Reiner: "All that counts is that you make a high quality, excellent game. Your profession, money, background, everything else doesn't count. Everything you need will follow if you make a good game. Don't start out thinking about big money. Don't start thinking about self-publishing either. You should get a publisher. Publishers are very good at judging games. If a publisher doesn't want your game, probably no one else will either.

"Designing games is a long learning process. You need to get experience by playing lots of different games, talking to people who make and play games, and studying the product lines of companies. I've done games for 35 years and I'm still learning all the time. I still understand very little about what makes a game successful. You can look back on past products and do marketing analysis for explanations of why a game was successful or not. That's all very nice, but it's irrelevant to understanding what's going to succeed in the future."

Brian: "Is there any more advice you'd like to give new inventors?"

Reiner: "Do what you do best. Follow your own path. Develop your own style. Also, clarify why you are doing it. You need to know your own reason. My reason is in my motto: 'Bringing enjoyment to the people.' That's why I design games, and for me, that's the only thing that counts."

23

Chapter 6

Interview With a Publisher

Mike Gray

Mike Gray

Mike Gray is Senior Director of Product Design for Hasbro games, the biggest game company in the world. Mike's division, which includes Milton Bradley and Parker Brothers, produces approximately one million games a week—more games than most companies sell in a year! Originally a game designer himself, Mike has evaluated and developed hundreds of successful products throughout his 23 years at the company.

Mike isn't just a corporate suit—he's famous for his love of playing games and readily admits that although it can be tough, working at Hasbro is a dream job.

Brian: "What are some of your favorite games to play?"

Mike: "Oh man, there are a lot. *Magic* is a great game, I love it. That's probably my favorite if I had to pick one. *Carcassonne, Mystery Rummy #1. Battle Line* by GMT is a great two player card game by Reiner Knizia."

Brian: "How do you recognize a good game when you see it?"

Mike: "When I see it or when I play it? There's a difference. As a product acquisition guy there are a bunch of things you have to take into account apart from how well it plays. For example, will it appeal to the target market before they get a chance to play it? Visual appeal is really important. You could design the best game on Earth and if it looked like checkers, people just aren't going to be drawn to it. There are lots of great games that just look hard and dull—they don't look alive. They look like work.

"Remember that if a product gets TV advertising we have 30 seconds to get the idea across and almost all the information there is visual. Plus visual appeal is what people are using to make a judgment when they're looking at a product in the store. Most of our products are very physical. There are very few flat board games being introduced in the mass market. Now I love flat board games. I have hundreds or maybe over a thousand in my basement, but they just aren't right in today's marketplace unless they really have something special.

"Another thing we look for is a gimmick—I don't know what else to call it. It might be a randomizer, a mechanism, something that shoots out maybe, as long as it's relevant to the game. Maybe it's some kind of moving parts, like a donkey that kicks or a car that makes noises, something to give the product some life. Sometimes we see that and say 'Wow, that's awesome!'"

Brian: "You said there's a difference between when you first see a game and when you play it. What do you look for when you play it?"

Mike: "It has to be easy to get into. It can't be the same as something I've played before. It has to be fun and challenging. It should be competitive. It should have a little bit of luck. Luck provides some suspense. With luck you don't have complete control over the game so there are always surprises. Luck also tends to broaden the age range of players. No luck means the game is solely dependent on thinking. You have to throw your whole mental self into it if there's no randomness. Most people want to play a game to relax. They don't want a game that's like 'Hey, let's take a test!'
    "Another thing I look for is some kind of a catch-up feature. If I roll all sixes or if I'm the best chess player, you just lose. That's no fun. There should be a way for someone who's behind to still have a shot at winning. The game shouldn't be too complicated, too long, and it shouldn't be too hard to figure out what to do. Some games give you a hundred options every turn. Most people are happy with about

25

three choices. The game has to have good rules. They should be short, fun to read, logically organized, and have examples.

"Unfortunately, good games don't always sell. There are good games that bomb. There are lots of reasons why. It might have terrible packaging, a bad theme, an awful TV commercial, there might be similar games that are just better, it might come out too late for the buying seasons, or it might be too expensive. All things beyond the inventor's control."

Brian: "Can you tell me about a successful product you looked at and what made it so good?"

Wheels on the Bus

Mike: "Sure. *Wheels on the Bus* was a kids' game that did a great job on all of the points I talked about. It had a great theme—a well-known nursery rhyme. It had terrific visual appeal and good packaging, with a clear window that let you see the bus itself. It was priced right. It had a good name, so you know what it's all about as soon as you hear it. If you know the rhyme you already know the game play is about the wheels, the doors, the wipers, etc., so it's easy to figure out what to do. The game play was fun. It had great appeal to the preschool market and it was an excellent seller."

26

Brian: "What mistakes should new inventors avoid when designing a new game?"

Mike: "A big problem is when you fall in love with your own idea so you no longer have an objective view of it. You've been hearing all this praise from your friends, but none of it's objective.

"Novices will design a game for themselves—something they want to play. That's fine, but if you want to make money you have to sell a lot of them. So there had better be a lot of 'you' around to buy them. Otherwise you need to learn to design for other kinds of people. Other ages especially. The age of your target players determines a lot of things about your game. The cost, the length of play, the amount of strategy are all dependent on players' ages. The first thing you need to do is figure out who it's for.

"Novices need to study the catalogs of the companies they're pitching to. If you can customize your product to a need of that company you're a whole lot closer to making a sale. Hasbro is a wholesome company with games that parents see as safe and having benefits. So when we see a game idea that has to do with drinking, for example, that's a big waste of time."

Brian: "What should people know about the actual presentation of an idea to a company?"

Mike: "In the rare occasion when a company keeps your game for evaluation, the prototype is going to have to do all the selling for you. At some point someone is going to evaluate your game when you're not there to smile and point out all the great features. Your game just sits there and doesn't say a thing. If it's not inviting, if it breaks, if the rules aren't clear and complete, your game is in trouble.

"When you're presenting, it's important to listen. You'll have all these reasons why it's great and all these testimonials from your grandma, but when they say it's too long, or it's red and it should be green, listen and write it down. You may get another chance to get it right.

"Be professional. New guys very often just don't know how. It's about listening, bringing good quality materials and spell-checked rules. Don't push too hard. Ask questions. Say 'thank you very much' and when it's done, hope they'll want to see you again instead of getting mad that they turned your idea down."

Brian: "How much do inventors make when you buy an idea?"

Mike: "We pay royalties at about 5% of wholesale sales. If it uses a licensed property like Disney or The Simpsons, the royalty will be more like 3% since we have to pay licensing fees."

Brian: "What's the review process like?"

Mike: "We look at tons of ideas. The initial review is the beginning of a year-long process for our two sales seasons, June and November. A game has to go through a bunch of R&D, Sales & Marketing reviews, and other meetings until it gets manufactured. A card game might take only 3 to 4 months, whereas a product with plastic parts might need 14 to 16 months. About a year is a good rule of thumb."

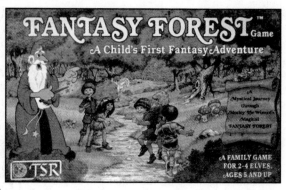

Fantasy Forest, an early Mike Gray game

Brian: "Why doesn't Hasbro look at game submissions from the general public?"

Mike: "If we did, there would be a line in front of the building. In our experience, games from novices tend to be things we're already working on or copies of other games, and the amount of good stuff is just really low. It would take a ton of time to sort through them all and it's just not worth it. When we get a submission, we just send it back unopened. Plus there are legal issues. The liability is a nightmare. Some people have their one baby they've been working on forever and if we look at it, they're going to think anything like it in the next several years was stolen from them. I've been at this company 23 years and nobody here is a crook. We don't steal ideas. But the public tends to be suspicious anyway. We were once sued for supposedly stealing this guy's idea of a round board for a board game. As if he was the only one ever to think of that. Ridiculous."

Brian: "What other advice do you have?"

Mike: "You have to figure out what the company is looking for. We're not going to post what we're looking for on the side of our building or even tell you on the phone because you might be working for Mattel. It's your job to figure out what we need, get an agent, and show it to us.

"Brokers are an important part of the process for us. They're our primary tool for filtering out the junk and getting to the good stuff. If you pay attention to all the points I talked about here and have a great idea, you really should get a broker and have them bring it to Hasbro first. Hasbro has the best sales, the best distribution, and the best marketing in the world."

SECTION TWO

HOW THE INDUSTRY WORKS

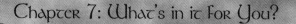

Chapter 7

What's In It For You?

Good Reasons to Publish a Game

Good Reason #1: It's Fun

Inventing a game is a cool experience. People in the game industry are interesting, friendly, intelligent, and love to have a good time. Game inventors get to make friends with great people and play games 'til they drop. It's exciting to see your creation change from a stumbling collection of rules to an elegant, smooth-running game. As your design skills improve it's amazing how much you learn about human nature, how people think, and what motivates them.

For me, the most personally rewarding aspect has been seeing my family, friends, and even strangers having a great time because I created a game. My mother called me up a few weeks ago and said "We all played your game last night. I haven't seen your grandmother laugh so hard in twenty years." It's no exaggeration to say that phone call alone would have been enough reward for all the work I did, even if the game hadn't made a cent.

Good Reason #2: To See Your Name in Cardboard

Let's not fool ourselves. Like it or not, the most common reason people want to get games published is to gratify their egos. Imagine how good it feels to show people a published game and say, "I created this." It's a way of sharing your imagination with others the same way an author or filmmaker does. In my opinion, this is a perfectly good reason to try to get your game published.

"Vanity press" is the nickname for games that aren't going to sell many copies, but someone wanted to publish anyway. Especially if you have a game that appeals to a very narrow segment of people, it can be cool to put together a game that a large company would never be willing to do. It's a fun way to get recognition within that hobby group and bring gaming to people who otherwise wouldn't play games.

Though vanity press companies are the peasants of the industry, they have a tradition of producing emperors. TSR, Wizards of the Coast, and others started out as vanity press companies with something in common—they weren't afraid to print games that might lose money.

Good Reason #3: You've Got the Curse

I've met many successful game inventors, and one characteristic I see again and again is the inability to stop thinking of ideas. If you've got this kind of drive you almost have no choice but to go into game inventing. "I think about new games constantly," says Brian Hersch, inventor of *Taboo*. "In the car, in meetings, it never stops."

When asked about the most important traits for being a good

30

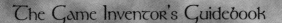

game designer in an interview on the Web site: www.discovergames.com, Reiner Knizia replied, "You maybe have to be a little bit mad. Games are never out of my head. I am constantly thinking 'is this a topic for a game?'" Reiner usually has about 100 games at once in various stages of completion and in his head.

Mike Fitzgerald, designer of *Wyvern* and *Mystery Rummy*, has it too. "My mind can't sit still. There's never a time when my brain isn't working on something," he admits.

If you're lucky (or unlucky) enough to be one of the few people with Game Inventor's Curse, you probably already have several games in your head or on paper. Take heart. You're in good company.

Bad Reasons to Publish a Game

Do people really spend enormous amounts of time and money inventing games that are the most annoying, difficult, and staggeringly boring abominations ever to disgrace cardboard? Do they ever!

Bad Reason #1: Your Friends Don't Want to Hurt Your Feelings

In late 2000, a woman submitted a cover letter and her prototype of a board game to Wizards of the Coast. She had spent countless hours and hundreds of dollars on the artwork and prototype, even going so far as to hire a lawyer to patent and trademark the game, which she proudly pointed out in her cover letter. The letter then spent a couple of pages gushing about how great the game was. Her friends and family loved it. They rated it 10 out of 10 in every category they could think of. She asked them to try to find some fault with it, but they just couldn't. Finally, one of them burst out with "The only thing I don't like about it is that I didn't think of it myself!" Any guesses on our reaction? The only reason publishers finish reading letters like this is the same reason motorists slow down to watch gruesome accident scenes—morbid fascination. Beside the fact there was already a similar game on the market and beside the fact our company clearly stated we didn't publish board games at the time, the game was awful—it wasn't even remotely fun to play. The lesson here is a sad one: Don't trust your friends. At least don't rely on them as your sole source of feedback on game play.

Bad Reason #2: It Seems Easy

Shortly after their *Pokémon Trading Card Game* became the best-selling game of all time, Wizards of the Coast received a game submission I'll call "Z-Warriors of the Future." Z-Warriors was a card game with over 200 cards complete with artwork, graphic design, and rules text on each card; an enormous undertaking for any inventor. Part of Wizards' submission materials asked the inventor to explain some important aspects of the game. The completed submission questions read like this:

Q: What audience is this product intended for?
A: Same as *Pokémon*.
Q: Why will players like the game?
A: It's just like *Pokémon*.

31

Q: Why did you choose us as a publisher?
A: It's just like *Pokémon*.

Looking more closely at the game, it was indeed, exactly like *Pokémon*, with only the names, symbols, and artwork changed! The Wizards Research and Development crew was incredulous. This guy had spent a staggering amount of time rehashing a game Wizards already published, then submitting it to them hoping they would pay him royalties for it. If there was a competition for unrealistic expectations, this guy would've set a record. There is a lesson here for the rest of us though. Many assume that if a company has a successful game they should want another one just like it to make even more money. In fact the opposite is true. A second game that's too similar to the first uses up more resources (graphic designers, editors, marketing dollars) and is just as likely to pull players away from the first game as it is to bring in new ones. Marketers call this "cannibalization risk" because the new game risks eating up another game's customers.

Bad Reason #3: It's An Idea Whose Time Has Come...And Gone

If you've ever seen the face of an inventor realizing the game that consumed the last several months of his life is unmarketable, you'll understand why many publishers make themselves difficult to approach. One individual invented a game that really did have the right elements. It could easily have been a success . . .except for one problem. The first publisher he showed it to said, "Looks like *Settlers of Catan*." The inventor: "Settlers of Who?"

Publisher: "*Settlers of Catan*. Came out in Germany, won Spiel des Jahres (Germany's Game of the Year) in 1995, and sold over a million copies. It's almost exactly like your game."

The inventor could do nothing but slump down in his chair. He'd come up with a fantastic idea but someone else had beat him to it a few years earlier. This happens more often than you might think. The moral of the story is that inventors need to do their homework and check out what's already on the market before they start approaching publishers.

Bad Reason #4: To Get Rich

Very, very few inventors get rich. Those that do usually have to dedicate a big portion of their lives to developing and promoting the game over several years. Only a handful of people in history have been able to invent a game in their spare time and make enough to retire on without quitting their day jobs. On the bright side, many of them were willing to share their insights in this book.

To be clear, there is some money in game design. It's quite reasonable to make $5,000 or $10,000 a year in your spare time if you have some talent and perseverance. The great thing about games is that most publishers pay inventors on a royalty basis. That means if the game sells well, you do the work once, but get paid lots of times. If you have a couple of games out at the same time you can collect checks for quite a while without doing any more work at all.

Realistically, if your primary interest is in making money you should find a good mutual fund and avoid the game industry like the plague. It's risky, it's difficult, and you won't succeed unless you love it with all your heart.

INSIDER'S VIEW—ARE YOU A CRACKPOT?

Take this simple test and find out

Game companies are constantly on red alert for eccentrics who don't get it. All of these questions are based on statements made by actual crackpots trying to sell a game. Have you or other game inventors you know uttered these statements—True or False?

1. Publishers will be sorry if they don't buy my game.
2. My lawyers have registered my game with the U.S. Patent Office, Copyright Office, and Library of Congress so don't try to steal it.
3. I've been working on this idea night and day for eight years so you know it must be good.
4. My game will make millions. Publishers should be grateful I'm giving them the chance to be part of it.
5. I've also invented a watermelon peeler and hamster shampoo that no one wants to manufacture either.
6. My board game based on my experiences in prison will be popular because people are fascinated by the interesting world of prison life.
7. I don't feel comfortable showing it to you for security reasons, but you have to trust me, my game is really, really good.
8. It's based on technology that hasn't been developed yet, but all you have to do is send me some electrical engineers and I'll tell them how to invent it.
9. I'm actually the one who first thought of *Trivial Pursuit* and *Magic: the Gathering* before they were released, so you know my next idea will be good.
10. It's the next *Monopoly*.

33

Chapter 8

How New Games Happen

Design

All new games start with someone's bright idea. The good news is that most game design companies don't have a staff of full-time inventors creating new games. It's usually more cost-efficient for them to buy or license at least some amount of games from independent inventors (that's you)! Inventors, often called designers, drive the whole creative process. They take the germ of an idea and play around with it until it's a working game. They create a prototype and test it out with lots of players, collect feedback, and make numerous revisions until it's ready to sell.

Pitching

The designer's next step is to convince a publisher to risk his money getting the game manufactured. It's a sad truth that just like movies, books, and music, the game industry is overflowing with people who think they're more talented than they really are. For that reason, the most desirable publishers have to screen out the hacks and protect themselves from the crackpots. You need to demonstrate you're a legitimate prospect and have some talent before your game even reaches the reviewer's desk. When you finally do get the chance to make your pitch you need to put yourself in the other guy's shoes for a moment. Here's the question a publisher asks himself when looking at your game: "Am I willing to risk losing $20,000 if this game doesn't sell?"

Manufacturing

When a publisher gives the go-ahead to publish a new game, he hands it off to his art department. Once the art and graphic design are finished, the rules are edited, and all the final touch-ups are complete, the game goes to production. The production people select what kind of paper and plastic are going to be used for each component and convert the artwork from computer files or photographs to films, which are fed into the printing machines at the factory. The presses churn out boxes, boards, and cards, the molds spit out the pieces, and a worker puts them all together and shrink-wraps it. Once the entire print run is complete, it goes on a truck.

Distribution

Once the game is on a truck it needs to get to stores. The very largest publishers can call up the largest chain retailers like Toys R Us and ask how many copies they want, but what about all the small publishers and small retailers? There are about 5,000 game and hobby stores in North America that aren't part of any chain. It doesn't make sense for a small publisher to call each store up and ask if they want to carry a few games. Likewise, a retailer that carries fifty different games doesn't want to call fifty publishers and write fifty checks every time he places an order. This is where the distributors come in. Distributors buy games from publishers, store them in a warehouse, mark them up about 50%, and send retailers a catalog from which to order.

Retailing

When a shop owner puts your game on a shelf in her store, it's called retailing. Retailers pretty much fall into two major categories: mass market retailers and specialty/hobby shops. Mass market retailers are generally composed of big department stores like Target, Wal-Mart, and the 800-pound gorilla of the industry, Toys R Us. Toys R Us alone accounts for 19% of all tabletop game sales. Hobby shops, on the other hand are usually small stores privately owned and run by dedicated people who love games (and/or comic books).

INSIDER'S VIEW— INVENTOR: BRIAN HERSCH

Brian Hersch is one of the giants of the American mass-market board game category. He has turned out numerous hits (licensing 35 different games), personally inventing not one, but two best-selling games now considered modern classics in the industry. *Outburst* has sold over 13 million copies since its release in the 1980s. His second huge hit, *Taboo*, has also reached the 13 million mark, but in nearly half that time. You can find both of these titles on the shelves of any large American retail chain that sells games. Brian Hersch is a confident and charismatic man with a somewhat paradoxical personality. He loves to play around endlessly

Brian Hersch

with games, but has zero tolerance for nonsense in his business dealings.

In 1984 Brian was a successful real estate developer who also happened to be a phenomenal *Trivial Pursuit* player. The success of the new category fascinated Brian and he noticed the glut of other companies trying fruitlessly to replicate the product's success. It was clear to him that these other publishers just didn't get it. Brian recalls, "*Trivial Pursuit* was really an opportunity for people in a certain age range, many with liberal arts educations, to

36

use all the pop cultural memories they had absorbed over the last generation. It wasn't about intelligence or knowledge, it was about reliving the shared experiences of that generation's youth." Seeing all these game professionals completely miss the point of such a huge phenomenon convinced Brian that he could do well in the industry.

Brian's first game was called *Out of Context*. He pitched the game to Selchow & Righter, publishers of *Trivial Pursuit*, and they were impressed enough to accept it on the spot. Riding high on their unprecedented success, Selchow & Righter's managers took their time putting a contract together and repeatedly haggled over details. Most unpublished inventors would have looked at such an opportunity with the hottest publisher in the business as a once-in-a-lifetime chance, but Brian was so confident in his ability to turn out hit games that he stood firm in his contract negotiations. After the fourth draft of the contract, Selchow executives tried to squeeze Brian over the terms, telling him, "Sign it now, or we're done and you'll never get to Toy Fair next month." To their disbelief Brian walked away from their offer.

Brian took the game to the next New York Toy Fair himself. Being an outsider to the industry, he was unable to secure a spot in the main exhibit hall so he rented a storeroom in an adjacent building. Despite all odds, his game was strong enough to attract many of the biggest publishers, and he quickly placed the game with Western Publishing. The game sold close to half a million copies, an unqualified success for any first-time inventor. This success also opened many doors for further submissions.

Driving through the canyons of Los Angeles during a rainstorm one night, Brian was headed home for a dinner party. His mind wandering, he happened to notice a radio program talking about an anniversary celebration of the Battle of the Bulge. "It's the kind of thing you don't think about very often, and I started wondering how much I knew about it," Brian recounts. When he arrived at the party, he walked into the house and said "Everyone name 10 things about the Battle of the Bulge!" This entertainment lasted the whole evening and thus was born the core mechanic of *Outburst*.

Taboo was inspired by a game in a TV show run by friend and TV celebrity Dick Clark, whom Brian met when they did business on *Out of Context*. Once he put the basics of the game together, he took his time perfecting it until he felt it was ready to sell. By this time Brian was recognized as one of the top inventors of the industry and had no problem getting meetings with publishers. He recalls the story of selling *Taboo*:

"Larry Bernstein, the Vice President of Marketing at Milton Bradley, came to my office to look at my new product ideas. During the meeting, my assistant handed me a note to step outside for a phone call that I wouldn't want to take in front of Larry. It was from the Vice President of Parker Brothers. (Milton Bradley and Parker Brothers are currently both owned by Hasbro, but were rivals at the time.) He had called up to tell me he didn't think *Taboo* was that good, didn't think it would ever be popular, and Parker Brothers didn't want it. I thanked him, walked back into the room, and pulled out *Taboo* to show to Larry. In two minutes *Taboo* was sold to Milton Bradley." *Taboo* turned out to be one of the most successful adult party games in history. Brian is currently taping a TV game show version of *Taboo*.

Taboo

Chapter 9

Anatomy Of A Publisher

L et's say you invent a game destined to become the next huge hit of the decade and take it to a large publisher. Here's what happens:

1. You or your agent gets the product in front of the concept acquisitions manager. He's impressed with the game and thinks it could be big.
2. He takes it to the developers in research and development and gets their opinions after they play it. They think it might be less work than the other projects that came through last week so they give it the thumbs up and agree it could be an instant classic.
3. The concept acquisitions manager takes the game to this month's R&D or marketing vice president who, in some cases, is also occasionally capable of recognizing a decent game.
4. The VP gives it the stamp of approval and the game is assigned to a marketing manager (sometimes called a product manager). The marketing manager's job is to figure out how many copies they will need to sell in order to spend some money on advertising and have some left over to make a profit. She consults with the production manager to find the cheapest way to manufacture it.
5. Once she has all the financial figures worked out, she'll have an approval meeting with representatives from the marketing department. They'll discuss things like whether or not it conflicts with any other games in the company's product line, how important it is to capture the consumers at which it's aimed, which of them already thought of this idea ages ago, and so forth.
6. When they all agree the game has great potential and won't take customers away from any of their other products, the marketing manager can put the game on the production schedule. From there it gets assigned to a graphic gesigner who converts your greasy napkin-scribblings into a professional-looking game.
7. While this is happening those frisky developers will play it some more looking for problems and improving the rules somewhat.
8. When they finish, the game is manufactured, distributed, and purchased by game-hungry consumers. A jaw-dropping royalty check graces your mailbox soon after.

Cast Of Characters

Keep in mind that in smaller companies one person may be performing several of these duties, but all these jobs have to get done one way or another. The largest companies may even have several people in some of these positions.

Agent

An agent is a professional game broker and is not affiliated with the company you're pitching to. He has a proven track record of bringing successful products to big publishers. Companies are willing to look at the games he recommends on a regular basis. Without an agent you will have to do all the work of selecting, researching, contacting, and visiting publishers yourself, and you still won't even be able to get into the biggest ones at all. On the downside, an agent typically charges 30% to 60% of your royalties. Agents are recommended for games aimed at the mass market, are sometimes recommended for games aimed at the hobby game and European markets. They are not recommended for the specialty game market.

Concept Acquisitions

Only the biggest companies have a concept acquisitions manager. In most other cases the head of creative services or even the president performs this role. This person's job is to seek out the best inventors while keeping the crackpots away. Usually he's under direction from the marketing department to specifically look for games aimed at a certain market segment. ("Why don't we have any games for teenage girls/country music fans/stamp collectors?") If you have an agent, this is the guy he meets with every so often to pitch your game along with half a dozen others.

Game Developers (a.k.a. Research and Development a.k.a. R&D)

These are the real game experts. Typically they know the products in the industry backwards and forwards. They have played more games than most people have ever heard of. Unfortunately, game companies have a spotty record when it comes to hiring in this area. Some companies are lucky enough to hire world-class talent while others scrape by with essentially incompetent developers. In any case, their job is to play your game and make an evaluation on whether or not it meets the company's needs, and more importantly, whether or not it's fun. If the company does accept your game, their next job will be to endlessly playtest it and look for any problems you might have overlooked in the rules or play balance. It's actually a very difficult job and requires the ability to perform analysis on several levels simultaneously.

Graphic Designer

The graphic designer can be the inventor's best friend or worst enemy. The designer creates all the artwork for the entire game, from board and card layouts all the way to the product logo and box top. Larger companies will assign one of their own graphic designers to come up with a look and feel for your product. In most cases you won't have any say in the matter if they decide to make the box green with purple spots. With a smaller company you may be expected to hire a graphic designer yourself. This can get expensive but you'll have greater control over the final art.

Marketing Manager

The marketing manager is ultimately responsible for making sure the game's sales revenues are high, expenses are low, and there is some money remaining for profit. She decides how much to spend on advertising and promotions, how much they can afford to spend on printing and components, and estimates how well the game is expected to sell. Since she holds the checkbook, she's in charge—everyone follows her direction with the game. She even determines how much time graphic designers and R&D can spend working on the project because their salaries for each hour devoted to the game are ultimately traced back to her project's budget.

Production Manager

The production manager's job is to figure out the cheapest way to get the product printed at the desired level of quality. The marketing manager starts by giving him specifications on what kind and quality of components the game will have. He gets prices on each component: plastic pieces, a board, rules, the box, etc. Based on those costs, the marketing manager figures out how many copies they can afford to print, then places the order. The production manager then arranges for the games to be printed and shipped to the distributors.

Marketing And/Or Sales Department

Yes, in addition to all of the above, your game has to impress a bunch more people you don't know. Each person in this department has responsi-bility for a certain product or group of products and is trying to figure out if your game is: a) going to be easy to sell and b) a good strategic fit for the company (meaning it won't steal customers away from their other games). It's actually functions like a big chain. Retailers are trying to guess what kinds of games customers want. Distributors are trying to guess what retailers want. The sales and marketing department are trying to guess what the distributors want. And now you, at the end of this chain, should be trying to figure out what the sales and marketing people want.

Boss Or Vice President

Residing somewhere at the top of all this is an executive who's going to take credit if your game does well and risk losing his reserved parking spot if it tanks. Executives hate that since the early people take the good parking spots and having to park far away proves that they come to work at 9:45 a.m.

INSIDER'S VIEW— PUBLISHER: R&R GAMES

R&R Games is a small but quickly growing company that operates mainly in the American specialty games market, but whose products clearly have mass market potential. With 12 games currently on the shelves and several more in development, the company sells around 75,000 games a year. R&R's *Time's Up!* is one of my all-time favorite party games, and one I recommend inventors check out. I spoke with founder and president of R&R Games Frank DiLorenzo about how the company publishes new products.

Brian: "How many game concepts do you look at each year?"

Frank: "Hundreds. Probably something like 500 a year."

Brian: "How many of those 500 actually get published?"

Frank: "Well, every game gets a cursory glance.

Frank DiLorenzo

Maybe 100 make it past that first screening. About two dozen make it to the stage where we playtest them. And of those, about three games a year will make it to market."

42

Brian: "How do you recognize a game that has potential for success?"

Frank: "It has to be fun. It can't be too complex, 'cause I just don't have the patience. It's got to have interaction. You don't want everyone playing solitare at the same table. There need to be important decisions that lead to cause and effect. It needs social interaction. If there's laughing, that's really good."

Brian: "What are the biggest mistakes inventors make?"

Frank: "They copy other games—either intentionally copying them or unintentionally because they didn't do any homework. I get enough Monopoly clones to choke a horse. Big waste of time. Another thing is too many components. People don't understand the concept of price point. They don't realize what it takes to manufacture all those pieces. Extraneous items are expensive, they usually detract from the game, and don't add to the fun. Inventors also make the games too complex. They bury the fun parts of the game under too many rules."

Brian: "What's the review process like?"

Frank: "I will only look at a synopsis to begin with. I won't look at a prototype unless I asked the inventor to send it. I give the synopsis a quick read. If there's any interest I will ask for the prototype and take a look at it. We test prototypes in-house in March through June. We have several groups of friends and co-workers that we like to use for playtesting. I have detailed forms that they fill out to evaluate each game they play. The next step is to give it to the external playtesters. We have between 30 to 50 playtesters around the country that we send the games to. They rate all the games we send them and the highest rated games are the most likely to get published."

Brian: "Once you give a game the thumbs up, how long does it take to get on a store shelf?"

Frank: "Anywhere from 6 months to 2 years. The simpler the game is the faster it gets through the process. It just takes longer for complex games and for games that need a lot of artwork."

Brian: "How complete do you expect a submission to be in terms of art, editing, and playtesting?"

Frank: "As long as it's a playable prototype, I don't care what it looks like."

Brian: "What advice would you give to new inventors?"

Frank: "Do research. Learn about how games are manufactured

43

so you understand what components you really want. Test your game thoroughly! Get people who aren't your family or friends to test it. If you want, you can go to the mall and see if you can get people to talk to you about the game. Do people who don't know you get interested?

"Another thing inventors should know is patents are a waste of time and money. They are useless. When you talk about your game's patent it shows you aren't familiar with the industry. Also watch out for agents that review games. There are some legitimate agents out there, but there are a lot more who will just take your money and give you nothing. I see that all the time. You have no way of knowing whether or not they showed your game to publishers. Watch out if they are trying to charge you $800 up front instead of a percentage of sales."

R&R Games

44

Chapter 10

Markets For Games

From an inventor's perspective, there are basically four markets (categories) in which to sell games. They're defined by the type of consumer who buys the games in that market, methods of distribution, and product expectations of the publishers. The categories are mass market, hobby games, American specialty games, and European games.

Mass Market

Mass market games are the most recognizable of all games to most Americans. They're the ones you see on the shelves of Wal-Mart, Toys R Us, and KB Toys. They are usually one of two types. The first type is adult party games like *Pictionary*, *Taboo*, and *Cranium*. Alongside these newcomers are the venerable classics and family games that many of us grew up with, such as *Monopoly*, *Clue*, *Life*, *Boggle*, and *Scrabble*. Most young children's games fall into this category too. Any game on these shelves has some big names to compete with, but many new ones do it each year. The most successful ones become modern classics.

Hobby Games

Hobby games are mostly the domain of males in their teens and twenties who play religiously every week or more. In general these games are extremely complex and it's not unusual for fans to spend hundreds of dollars a year buying supplements, cards, figurines, or new rulebooks for a single game. Hobby games fall into three major categories: role-playing games, miniatures games, and trading card games.

American Specialty

This is sort of a catchall category for American games that aren't mass market or hobby games. It includes products targeted at a certain segment, such as strategy games, drinking games, "How to Host a Mystery" games, and so forth. Generally you should expect small print runs from small publishers, but it's definitely the easiest category to get started in. There are also a number of games in this category that would be appropriate for the mass market, but for one reason or another haven't gone through that distribution channel (yet).

European

When someone talks about the European game market, they're mostly talking about games published by German companies. The German game market is a big one. In Germany games seem to be quite a bit more popular as a mainstream entertainment choice when compared to North American tastes. German companies put out dozens and dozens of new games each year, only a small fraction of which ever get translated and make it over to the United States. German games in general tend to be much more complex, abstract, and strategic than most Americans are used to. That's part of the appeal for customers in this market.

Others

These four markets are by no means the only places you can sell games. If you have a football game and you can get sporting goods stores to carry it, or if you can find some other way to skip traditional game retail outlets, that's great. Some companies sell directly to the consumer by mail order. Others sell on eBay or via a Web site. There's also a modest amount of sales to educational distributors and schools. There are innumerable other options for getting your game into consumer's hands. However, as of yet, none of them have been able to generate sales figures that come close to those of the four traditional markets.

This section wouldn't be complete without a quick word on computer games. In the last ten years computer game development has advanced so rapidly that it almost always takes a couple of years and millions of dollars to launch and market a new title. Because these companies have so much invested in each new title, and each company works on relatively few at a time, they have much more incentive to design game concepts themselves. Though there may have been a market for computer game ideas in the early 1980s, there really isn't one now.

INSIDER'S VIEW—
PUBLISHER: PATCH

Brothers Fran and Bryce Patch started a successful printing company in Beloit, Wisconsin in 1971. They found that much of their business came from manufacturing games for other companies, including *Trivial Pursuit* boards. In 1985 they decided to start printing their own products, beginning with children's puzzles, and moving in to adult board games with *TriBond* in 1992. Building on *TriBond*'s success, the company launched many other top-selling games in the following decade such as *Mad Gab*, *Malarkey*, and *Blurt*. Patch also entered the Christian products market in 1997 with Bible-themed versions of many of its most popular products.

Today, the modest-sized company of about 100 employees is frequently among the top three sellers in the mass market games business.

I spoke with Peggy Brown, Vice President of Product Development at Patch, about how the company produces such big-selling titles and what they look for in a game.

Brian: "Being a top mass market manufacturer, can I assume you don't look at game ideas from the general public?"

Peggy: "We actually are a little unusual in that we do look at unsolicited submissions from people who request an inventor's packet. *Tribond* and *Mad Gab* both came from people that solicited the company and turned out to be our biggest products. You just can't put up a firewall if you want a chance at the next big idea."

Brian: "What should first-time game inventors watch out for?"

Peggy: "They don't understand what it costs to make a game. Sometimes we'll open the game box and think, 'ok, this could retail for about $300.' There are too many complicated components. They don't understand how games are manufactured and sold.

"Another thing we see is that people invent to their own specialized interests. Lawyers think law is fascinating, so they invent lawyer games. Real estate agents invent real estate games. They don't realize the general public probably isn't as interested in the subject as they are.

"Often if there's some big world event, we see games based on that theme. After the tragedies of September 11, 2001, we saw a bunch of submissions based on world maps and catching terrorists. They don't realize that it's not like a product based on a movie release. It takes up to a year to get a product on the market and by that time, the event is no longer a hot topic."

Brian: "What are some of the good things you look for in game submissions?"

47

Peggy: "We have to know where we can sell it. There are so many hurdles a game has to pass. Is it feasible to manufacture at a reasonable price? There's a basic conflict that happens with all new games since it has to be different enough to be new and exiting, but similar enough to other games that people recognize what it is. If it's too different you have to spend huge amounts of marketing money trying to tell people what it is. If it's too similar, nobody will be interested."

Brian: "Can you tell me about a successful product you looked at? What made it successful?"

Peggy: "One thing that worked well was to give a request. We talked to the professional inventing community about what we were looking for. We have a radio challenge program in which we have a network of radio stations that play our games on the air with callers. It's a great marketing tool since we don't pay a nickel and it's better than advertising since they play it for more than 30 seconds and you hear real people having fun with it. We were looking for some more radio-promotable adult family board games. The inventors we talked to came up with five games that fit the format we were looking for and two of them are in next year's product line."

Brian: "What else should inventors know about the industry?"

Peggy: "If you're serious about it, don't be so attached to your idea. Some ideas are so specific you can't hope to hit the nail on the head with the first try. If you are too married to your idea that company won't work with you again because you're not flexible. I also recommend using agents. It's true that if they sell your game, you won't get to keep all 5% of your royalty. But 5% of zero is still zero.

"Don't mortgage your house. The odds of having a big hit are very low. There are things about the business that just take a long time to learn. You can't know them until you have experience."

GAMES AND COMPANIES YOU SHOULD KNOW

Chapter 11

Mass Market Games You Should Know

Mass market games are mostly defined by where they are sold and who buys them. They are mainly sold in large chain stores. As for who buys them, if you look in the average family's cupboard, these are the games you're most likely to find. There are mass market games especially for kids (*Candyland*), adults (*Trivial Pursuit*), and teens (*Twister*). Typical shoppers in this category are very often moms looking for a gift item. As a rule, mass market games, especially the newer ones, are simple to understand and quick to get started playing. You should be able to figure out what to do within 30 seconds of opening the box.

The most well known games in this category, *Monopoly*, *Life*, and *Scrabble*,

A mass market game shelf

are best described as American classics. They are the games that gained so much momentum over many years that they became a part of American culture. Publishers agree that if *Monopoly* were invented today it would almost certainly never get off the ground. But because so many people have good memories of it, they buy it for

50

their kids and play it with them, creating new memories in a new generation and cementing its status as an American institution.

Beside the classics are the newcomers to the industry, some that are here to stay, and some destined to be short-lived fads. Here are the products you should play and companies you should know to have the necessary minimum game literacy in this market.

Monopoly (Parker Brothers)

The story you most often hear about *Monopoly*'s origin is that of Charles Darrow, an out-of-work Pennsylvania engineer. The story says Charles laid out an oilcloth on his kitchen table and put the game together using names taken from his memories of vacationing in Atlantic City. Darrow presented the game to Parker Brothers in 1934 and was immediately rejected. The team of executives identified 52 fundamental design errors in *Monopoly*. Further, they felt the game took too long to play and was too difficult to learn. Darrow decided to print and sell the game himself, and after he demonstrated the game's potential with solid sales, Parker Brothers took notice and bought the rights.

Monopoly board

The story you don't often hear is that of *The Landlord's Game* invented in 1904 by Lizzie Magie of Virginia. Her game, like *Monopoly*, had forty spaces, four railroads, two utilities, twenty-two properties for rent, with higher rent prices for a monopoly, and spaces called Jail, Go To Jail, Luxury Tax, and Parking. Lizzie's purpose in creating the game wasn't to have fun or make money—it was to promote political support for the "single tax theory," which said that government should base an individual's taxes on how much land he owned. Lizzie's game never went anywhere. No one knows specifically how Mr. Darrow came across it, but the evidence suggests Charles Darrow took more credit than he deserved for *Monopoly*.

In any case, the game was an unparalleled success for the floundering Parker Brothers Company. According to Robert Barton, an executive who was involved in reorganizing Parker Brothers, "It was a godsend. It rescued the business, which had come within an inch of disaster. The *Monopoly* game was definitely part of the Depression era. It let people fantasize that they could win in the real estate market."

Sales shot through the roof and within a year their factory was turning out 20,000 games each week. As Christmas approached, they received so many telegraphed orders that the clerks had to pack them in enormous laundry baskets stacked in the office hallways. With so many unfilled orders, the company finally called in a bookkeeping firm from Boston to help with the paperwork. The firm's agents walked in the door, saw the masses of unsorted papers in towering piles everywhere, and refused the job at any price.

Despite these unprecedented sales figures, Parker Brothers believed *Monopoly* was a fad that could only last a few years. In late 1936, company president George Parker himself gave the order to "cease absolutely to make any more boards or utensil boxes...we will stop making *Monopoly* against the possibility of a very early slump." But after sales leveled off, they suddenly shot up again, finally reaching a steady level well above that of any competing games. As parents taught it to their children, it remained popular through generations. More than any other game, it has attained the status of an American cultural institution.

Today *Monopoly* is the most well known commercial game in the world. It has been printed in 26 languages and has sold more than 100 million copies over its lifetime.

Many versions of Monopoly

The Game of Life (Milton Bradley)

In 1860 Abraham Lincoln grew a beard. Most took little notice, but for a lithographer named Milton Bradley the choice of facial hair was a disaster. Milton's most popular product had been a portrait of the clean-shaven Lincoln, and was rendered obsolete by the beard. In a desperate move Milton printed up the first copies of *The Checkered Game of Life* in 1860. It proved popular enough to save his business and establish him as a professional game manufacturer. One hundred years later, the Milton Bradley game company, now the top board game company in the world, asked inventor Reuben Klamer to design a game to celebrate the 100th anniversary of the company. Reuben could think of no better choice than an update of Milton's original success. The result is *The Game of Life*, a board game that has become one of the most popular games of the century and an interesting caricature of an idealized American lifestyle.

Life is an archetypal American classic family board game. Represented

by a peg in the driver's seat of a car, each player drives his way along the road-like game path. Players have minimal choices during game play, so that major life choices such as careers and kids just kind of happen willy-nilly. In fact there are only around a half-dozen strategic decisions for each player to make in the entire game. As players move through college, marriage, and children, (represented by additional pink and blue pegs in the car) they collect assets and try to save money for retirement. The winner is the player with the most cash value when everyone has retired. In spite of its mentality of consumerism (success in *Life* is measured by who has the most money when he dies), *The Game of Life* speaks to a wholesome, classic American need for children's entertainment. It's a game that

The Game of Life

parents feel good giving to kids and those kids later feel good passing to their kids.

Clue (Parker Brothers)

Anthony Pratt, a former law clerk, put the basic mechanics for *Clue* together with his wife in 1944 during his retirement near Bournemouth, England. It was several more years before the Pratts felt the game was ready to pitch, but they finally approached Waddington's Games in Leeds, England. Waddington's Managing Director Norman Watson played the game and immediately decided to publish it. It hit the stores in 1949 and was quickly picked up by publishing giant Parker Brothers. Today it remains one of the most popular games in the world.

Clue is a murder mystery board game where players represent suspects trying to discover who the killer is, where the crime occurred, and how it was performed. A killer card, a location card, and a weapon card are hidden in a secret envelope. The remaining cards are dealt to the rest of the players. Thus, each player has different information about which cards aren't in the envelope. During game play each player gets to look at some of the cards in other players' hands until someone is ready to make a guess at the three hidden cards, either because they've eliminated all other options, or because they hope to get lucky. An incorrect guess loses the game, a correct one wins it.

Clue is another example of a game that gathered so much momentum over the years that it became a cultural institution. The murder-mystery theme makes an appealing setting that fits well with the suspenseful nature of the game. *Clue* has an elegant deductive-reasoning mechanic that's unusual to find in the family board game market.

Scrabble (Hasbro & Mattel)

An unemployed architect from Poughkeepsie, New York named Alfred Butts put a crossword game together in the early 1940s using the front page of the New York Times to assign point values to letters based on the frequency of their appearance. He called the game Lexico and later changed it to Criss Cross Words. After the usual rejections from the large established publishers Alfred connected with James Brunot, a businessman with the insight to recognize the game's tremendous potential. They trademarked the name *Scrabble* in 1948 and began manufacturing sets out of an abandoned schoolhouse in Connecticut at the rate of 12 an hour. Although the game lost money at first, it steadily grew in popularity. According to legend, the president of Macy's Department Store discovered the game in the early 1950s and ordered it for his store. With this distribution power, the game quickly became a breakaway hit. After the publishing rights changed hands several times, the rights were strangely split up between the world's two biggest toy and game companies, with Hasbro getting the North American publication rights, and Mattel getting the rights to publish in the rest of the world. In any case, *Scrabble* remains the clear leader in the word game category to this day. More than 100 million sets have been sold worldwide and more than a million are sold each year in North America.

Part of the game's appeal is that everyone knows words. The game has the right amount of simplicity for anyone to start playing in minutes, but enough depth to keep serious players interested.

Scrabble

It's a clean mixture of strategic thinking (board placement) and language skill. *Scrabble* and *Boggle* together have such a dominant hold on the word game market that many publishers, even outside

54

the mass market, just aren't interested in looking at new word games.

Yahtzee (Hasbro)

An anonymous Canadian couple invented this fast-paced dice game on their yacht to play with guests. By 1956 enough friends wanted copies that the couple approached Edwin Lowe, a bingo card manufacturer, and asked him to print up some copies of *The Yacht Game* as gifts. Lowe saw a business opportunity and offered to buy the rights for the price of the first 1,000 games sold. As with many classics, it didn't move much its first year. Frustrated with poorly-performing advertisements, he hit on the idea of throwing "*Yahtzee* Parties," a marketing move that generated tremendous word-of-mouth advertising. The game took off soon after and Milton Bradley picked it up in 1973. Today it remains the best-selling dice game on the market.

Yahtzee is played with five standard dice and a scoresheet with 13 categories such as "full house," "straight," and so forth. Each turn a player rolls all the dice trying to get the highest total that matches any of her remaining categories. A player can reroll any of his dice up to two times before the turn is over and the player must record a score. Once the categories are filled, scores are added up and the highest wins.

Yahtzee

Dice are an interesting component of games. There's something mysteriously compelling about the tactile sensation of those small cubes that have such a big impact on one's destiny. Dice give players an unusually strong feeling of being connected to the game's outcome. If you ever watch kids throw the dice you'll notice that they if they rolled poorly they feel like it was because they didn't try hard enough. If they rolled well, they react as if it's because they were so skillful. It's a secret of perception that many game designs exploit. Rolling the dice is random chance, but it feels like a skill.

Uno (Mattel)

Ohio barbershop owner Merle Robbins created *Uno* in 1971. Merle started playing the game with his family, but when they and even their friends began playing *Uno* with increasing frequency, Merle realized he might have a game with good sales potential. He and his family put together $8,000 and had 5,000 copies of the game printed. Merle's retail success started when he began selling the game to customers in his barbershop. A few friends and local businesses picked up *Uno* and in spite of having no marketing, the game sold well through word of mouth. As *Uno* began to demonstrate its long-term potential, Merle decided to sell the game to someone with the money to help it really take off, a funeral parlor owner who believed in *Uno's* potential. He formed International Games Inc. to produce the game and sales took off. International Games created a strong niche market in family card games, a category largely ignored by other big publishers because prices were lower and it was hard to justify big marketing expenses.

Mattel acquired International Games in 1992. Today, *Uno* remains the best-known family card game in the mass market, with about 3 million units sold per year and over 100 million games sold since 1971. Many people don't realize that *Uno* is a variant of the traditional card game *Crazy Eights*, and essentially benefited from decades of playtesting in millions of households before its release.

The game's simplicity is what makes it appealing. It's easy to get started and there aren't many difficult decisions. Even little kids can do well against adults. The game moves at a lively pace and keeps the action going. It's a quick and engaging game with plenty of drama at the end.

Taboo (Hasbro)

Taboo is one of the most successful new adult party games of the '90s, selling more than 13 million copies since its release. Its inventor, Brian Hersch, got the basic idea from a segment of a TV show rehearsal he was attending with his friend, TV celebrity Dick Clark. Brian put the game together and, being an established professional inventor, pitched it directly to Milton Bradley, who snapped it up on the spot.

Taboo comes with a buzzer, a timer, and a stack of cards, each of which has a "guess word" and five "taboo words." Each turn, a player tries to get his teammates to say the guess word without saying any of the five forbidden words. If he does say a taboo word, an opposing team member (watching over his shoulder), buzzes him and the other team gets a point. For example, a player has to get his teammate to say "submarine" without saying "underwater, periscope, yellow, torpedo," or "boat."

Note the key elements that make this an excellent adult party game. It's easy to grasp the concept in seconds. It's interactive, with most of the players participating at every moment of play. It's fast-paced. It forces you to think on your feet and it feels good when you come up with a clever solution.

Trivial Pursuit (Hasbro)

Trivial Pursuit, whose origin is covered in detail earlier in the book, started the entire category of adult party games in 1983. In *Trivial Pursuit* players roll the dice and move wheel-shaped pieces around the board's circular path collecting pie-slice-shaped pieces from each of six trivia categories. When you land on a square you must answer a question from that category. A wrong answer ends your turn and a right one lets you roll again. Once your pie has collected a pie-slice from each of the

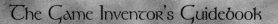

six categories, you can win.

Why was *Trivial Pursuit* such a runaway hit? My theory is that many of the questions give players an emotional payoff no matter what answer they give. For example, I believe in many cases the card writers will begin with an answer and then write the question. Take someone or something most people have heard of, such as world-famous chess player Bobby Fischer. He will be our answer. Next, look up some fact about his life and turn it into a question, such as "Who became the world chess champion in 1972?" a fact that very few people actually know. For most people, the only chess player they can think of is Bobby Fischer, so they're fairly likely to get it right with a wild guess. If they do, everyone is impressed that they knew such an obscure fact—even though they really didn't. Even if they don't get the answer right, when they hear it they recognize it and mentally give themselves credit for it. In their minds, people don't distinguish between "I've heard of the answer" and "I knew the answer." How many times have you heard people say "Oh, I knew that!" when they hear the right answer? Right or wrong, the designers have set you up to always feel smart with a question like that.

Mike Gray says that sometimes the question writers will put in a question that nobody is really expected to answer, but is such an interesting, unusual fact that they include it just as a conversation piece. Once a player hears the answer he can pull out that interesting tidbit of information at the next social gathering and seem smart to his other friends.

Trivial Pursuit

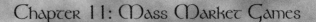

Pictionary (Hasbro)

Invented by Rob Angel, a 24 year-old Seattle waiter, and introduced in 1986, *Pictionary* was the next superstar game after *Trivial Pursuit* in the adult party games market. Rob himself went door-to-door, selling copies to local stores and generating grassroots enthusiasm for the game. As the game began to take off Rob became a partner in his own publishing company, scrambling to meet consumer demand. The game eventually made over $700 million and still sells about a million copies a year. Today *Pictionary* is published by Hasbro in the U.S. and by Mattel internationally.

Pictionary is sometimes described as visual charades. It comes with pads of paper and pencils and on your turn, it's your job to get your partner to say a target word by drawing pictures only—no letters or symbols. A successful try lets you advance on the board and next time it's your turn to guess.

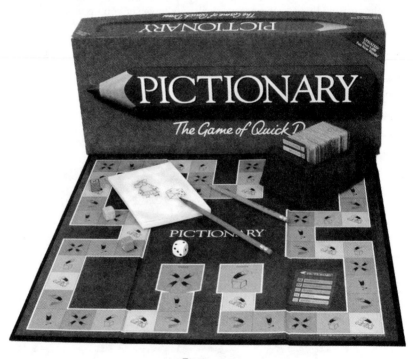

Pictionary

INSIDER'S VIEW— CRANIUM INVENTORS WHIT ALEXANDER AND RICHARD TAIT

In 1997 Richard Tait, a former Microsoft executive, returned home to Seattle from a weekend of playing board games in the Hamptons. Richard was intrigued by the fact that he was excellent at *Pictionary* but not at *Scrabble*, and on the plane home he began mentally designing a game in which teams of players would need multiple skills to win. Over breakfast at the Jitterbug restaurant, Richard pitched the idea to his former Microsoft co-worker Whit Alexander. Together, they assembled a team of designers including a journalist, a crossword-puzzle specialist, a college student, an art teacher, a mime, and a software editor. The two put up the money from their personal fortunes (Microsoft stock prices being what they were) for extensive testing, development, and the initial print run.

The game's hook is that it offers something for everyone to be good at. *Cranium's* game play is based on 14 various activities grouped into four categories: "Creative Cat, Data Head, Word Worm, and Star Performer." Teams face challenges to move their pieces on a board, selecting the team member they believe will be best at meeting the challenge. Challenges include drawing an object with your eyes closed, spelling words backwards, and sculpting objects out of clay.

Much of *Cranium's* success lies in its incredible distribution. Disdaining traditional markets like toy and game stores, they looked for places where "25- to 35-year-old dating yuppies" hung out. It so happened that Richard had recently climbed Mt. Kilimanjaro with a friend of Starbucks CEO Howard Schultz. They pitched the game to Howard, and soon *Cranium* was on the shelves of 1,500 Starbucks stores. They gave sample copies to Starbucks employees to play, generating fantastic word of mouth and frequent recommendations to customers. The two were also able to convince executives at such nontraditional outlets as Virgin Megastores and Barnes & Noble. *Cranium* sold more than a million units in 2001, making it one of the fastest-selling board games in U.S. history.

I spoke with Richard and Whit in their Seattle office.

Brian: "What drew you to the games business?"

Whit: "There were five things we had to think about when we first started putting this company together. First, we needed to figure out 'can you have a big hit board game?' There hadn't been one for about 15 years."

Richard: "We looked at the two biggest ones. *Trivial Pursuit* made about a billion dollars over its lifetime and *Pictionary* made about $750

59

million. That's more than almost any entertainment medium. Movies don't even make that much."

Whit: "The second thing we had to think about was startup costs. We looked at doing computer games, but that costs about $2 to $4 million to get started. We started *Cranium* with $110,000. So that tremendous upside coupled with the relatively low risk on the downside was interesting."

Richard: "Third, in 1998, when we were first putting this together, we saw a lot of smart people heading into dot coms. That's where all the innovation was taking place. But there wasn't any innovation going on in board games. Most of the stuff coming out was heavily licensed versions of the same old thing. There was an opportunity there—an innovative product would face very little competition.

"Fourth, we had to find out 'do people still want to play board games?' Is the play dynamic still sound? There hadn't been a hit for a long time. Was that because the time for board games was done? Clearly there was still a demand, but we weren't sure what to begin with.

"Fifth, we didn't have a better idea."

Whit: "It sounds funny to hear that but it's true. When Richard first came to me with the idea for a game, I said 'you're nuts!' But the thing is it's an incredibly strong core concept that had never been done before—a game everyone can excel at. It's a way they can look smart and funny, and be engaged and fully connected with one another."

Brian: "What makes your games different? How do you capture what other companies seem to miss?"

Richard: "Whit looked at historical play dynamics and what kinds of games had been successful in the past. We tried to figure out what worked and what else we could introduce that hadn't been done before. Howard Gardner, a Harvard psychologist, wrote the critical theory of multiple intelligences [Editor's note: Gardner's 1983 book is entitled, *Frames of Mind: The Theory of Multiple Intelligences* and was published by Basic Books]. It described several core human competencies—skills that society has valued from the earliest times. This gave us a rich framework to deliver on the promise of an experience where everyone shines.

"We have a 'moment-oriented' product development cycle. Our products are designed to celebrate, focus, and position a certain emotional moment. When you let a person show off their talents and skills, that moment is talked about for years to come. It's brought up at the next reunion. Really our product development is centered on a portfolio of moments we're trying to capture. Each of our products is aimed at a certain consumer with different needs.

"It's a novel approach to product development. Since our initial success we've been able to build on that known 'everyone shines' brand. Our products are successful because they meet the promise of an entertainment experience that will lighten and enlighten the players."

Brian: "Do you have any advice for new game inventors?"

Whit: "Get to prototype and playtest as soon as possible. We were playtesting within three weeks of starting out. Our early prototypes were seriously flawed and we could only find the problems during playtesting. Games evolve exponentially in very little time at this stage. You need to be honest with yourself. Listen as hard as you can. We used to change the playtest three times an evening as we responded to the players.

"Have orders before you go to manufacturing. We had a nervous month

Cranium

and a half where we realized we had missed Toy Fair and weren't sure if we would have any orders. You don't want that. Learn the critical points in the industry, such as when and where retailers buy games. Think about the specialty game market. The retailers there can help you sell. We originally intended to do regional distribution but we missed that opportunity when Starbucks wanted to take us nationally. But it makes a lot of sense to roll out regionally before you try to go national since you can build enthusiasm in your area.

"I don't want to be too sanguine about the risks in this business. You're looking at an industry where 50% of companies fail in the first year and another 50% in the second year."

Richard: "One more thing: if you have a strong concept and believe in it, don't take no for an answer. Everyone we talked to about our idea told us we were crazy. We didn't listen."

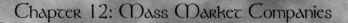

Chapter 12

Mass Market Companies You Should Know

Hasbro (Parker Brothers, Milton Bradley)

Hasbro's growth from a small family business into the undisputed ruler of the game industry is a fascinating story. Today Hasbro has yearly revenues of around $3 billion (about 50% games and 50% toys) and close to 10,000 employees worldwide, with roughly 40% of its sales coming from international markets. With a consistent history of buying up other successful game companies such as Milton Bradley, Parker Brothers, and Wizards of the Coast, Hasbro is by far the biggest game company in the world.

In 1923, Henry and Helal Hassenfeld, two brothers from Providence, Rhode Island, started a company called "Hassenfeld Brothers." Their first products were pencil boxes and school supplies. In 1943, Henry's son, Merrill, became president of the company and took the bold step of getting into the toy business with products like paint sets, crayons, and play doctor kits. Sales were good and the company became a major force in the growing toy industry. In the 1950s and 1960s, Hassenfeld Brothers brought out numerous iconic American toys, including Mr. Potato Head.

The idea of "dolls for boys" had long been ridiculed by industry experts, but in 1964 Hasbro created a new toy category by calling their fully-articulated military men "action figures" and introducing G.I. Joe. G.I. Joe turned out to be one of the most successful toy lines ever and brought tremendous growth to the company throughout the 1960s and 1970s. In 1968, Hassenfeld Brothers became a publicly traded company and changed its name to Hasbro. The 1980s were a period of acquisitions, as Hasbro bought companies with profits from their own properties like G.I. Joe: A Real American Hero, Transformers, and My Little Pony. In 1984, Hasbro bought Milton Bradley, the world's largest game company and with it, some of the best-known games in the world including, *The Game of Life*, *Candyland*, *Twister*, *Yahtzee*, and *Scrabble*. Alan Hassenfeld, grandson of founder Henry, became president of the company in 1989, and still runs the company today. In 1991, Hasbro acquired the Tonka Corporation, which owned Parker Brothers, the other titan of the games market. Continuing the pattern of acquisitions, Hasbro obtained *Pictionary*, *Clue*, and the electronic handheld game company Tiger Electronics. Finally, drawn to the continuing success of *Magic: the Gathering* and *Pokémon*, Hasbro bought Wizards of the Coast in 1998.

A visit to the Hasbro Games factory is a surreal experience. Unlike most game companies, that have all of their manufacturing done in the Asia, Hasbro maintains a 20-acre office and factory complex in Massachusetts. The smell of glue and ink pervade the air as dozens of huge machines spit out game boards 24 hours a day. Houses and hotels for *Monopoly* sets pour from a conveyor belt in a steady stream into a vast bin. Stamps with blades in the shape of jigsaw puzzle pieces cut thousands of sheets of cardboard as workers stand monitoring. The other end of the facility smells like baking bread, where the several-story-high automated Play-Doh machine molds the yellow cans and blows them through enormous cooling tubes onto moving conveyors. An adjacent machine spurts out a steaming hot cylinder of Play-Doh into each can as it races by. Nearby are huge presses printing three foot by three-foot sheets of money for games like *Life* and *Monopoly*. The floor foreman tells me they print more paper money here each year than the U.S. government.

Hasbro games puts out 40 or 50 new products each year, although many of them are extensions of their evergreen brands like *Monopoly*. Hasbro looks at around 16,000 new concepts each year. Of these, about 200 actually make it back to R&D, and around 40 are passed on to marketing. Of these, about 20 actually make it to market. Hasbro works exclusively with established game inventing professionals. If you want them to look at your game, you need an inside connection or a broker.

Mattel

In 1945, Ruth Handler, Elliott Handler, and Harold Mattson founded Mattel in a Southern California garage to produce picture frames. Looking for something to do with all the wood scraps left over from the picture frame manufacturing, Elliott hit on the idea of using them to build dollhouse furniture. Soon the dollhouse accessories were outselling the frames. After Mattson sold his interest in the company to the Handlers, they turned their full attention to manufacturing toys.

Business was good until a fateful moment in 1959 that changed the toy industry forever. Ruth noticed her daughter Barbara's excitement over playing with paper dolls and decided to try a plastic doll through which girls could live out their dreams. She called the doll "Barbie" in honor of her daughter. Sales exploded and Barbie turned out to be the best selling toy product in history. Mattel released Hot Wheels die cast cars in 1968. Together, these two brands helped Mattel become the biggest toy company in the world. Mattel is truly a huge company, with yearly revenues approaching $5 billion. Other big brands include Fisher-Price toys, Matchbox cars, American Girl dolls and books, and licensed Disney and Sesame Street items. About 50% of its revenues come from Wal-Mart, Toys R Us, and Target sales. In 1992, Mattel acquired International Games, and began publishing games like *Othello* and *Uno*.

Despite its huge size and dominant position in the toy business, Mattel has a relatively less aggressive attitude about the games market. Though it's consistently the number two company in mass market games, it puts out somewhat fewer game products than other companies in the industry, choosing to rely on its evergreen sellers. Mattel tends to regard its game division as one branch of the toy business.

With its place at the top of the toy industry food chain, Mattel is a prime target for the crackpot inventors of the world. It's not surprising that Mattel deals only with proven successful designers. First-time inventors will need to go through a broker to reach them.

Pressman

Founded in 1922 by Jack Pressman, Pressman Games is the third largest game manufacturer in North America. Jack's son, Jim, is the current president. Under his leadership the company has published many successful games, most notably those based on TV game show licenses, including *Jeopardy* and *Wheel of Fortune*. If you walk through the game aisle of your local mass market retailer, other Pressman games you're likely to see include *Mastermind*, *Rummikub*, *Tri-Ominos*, *True Colors*, and *Mindtrap*.

The company's headquarters are in New Brunswick, New Jersey, where they manufacture many of their products as well.

University Games

University Games is among the top five board game companies in the business, despite being a relatively new company, launched in 1985.

University Games positions its products as being focused on social interaction, entertainment, and education. On their Web site, company co-founder Bob Moog says, "The players need to watch what everyone is doing, knowing it will impact them, and then they have to react. It's an experience you can't get watching TV, reading a book, or playing on a computer. It has always been our goal to design games that challenge the intellect, bring out personalities, and stimulate imaginations and creativity." "And," says Moog, "Our focus is on superior playing games, not just games that will sell well because of TV advertising. Another thing we do is listen to the market. We sponsor an annual National Young Game Inventors Contest that brings in over 1,000 absolutely amazing entries. The diversity is incredible and provides unique insight into what excites today's kids. It's great market research and it's great fun." University Games publishes each year's winning game.

INSIDER'S VIEW— INVENTOR: GEORGE PARKER

George Parker was born just after the Civil War way back in 1867, in Salem, Massachusetts. As a teenager, he formed a gaming club with his friends to play checkers, chess, and dominoes. The group also found a game called *The Mansion of Happiness*, which also happened to be one of the first American board games ever published. The purpose of the game was to instill moral values in the impressionable minds of America's idle youth. George and his friends felt the game was too preachy and wished for a game that focused on fun, not sermonizing. George decided to create one.

During this era, playing cards were frowned on because of their association with gambling, so George based his game idea on a goal every American could support: making money. He called the game *Banking*. It consisted of 160 cards and a mechanic where players borrowed money from the bank, invested it, and hopefully paid it back to the bank with interest, with the richest player ending up the winner. His only real purpose in creating the game was to have something new to play in the club, and soon *Banking* became the group's favorite game.

In 1883, after endless playtesting, his friends convinced him to submit it to two book publishers in Boston. Although it was turned down, one of the publishers mentioned that George might try publishing the game with his own money. He was sixteen at the time and his life's savings amounted to $50. It was enough to print 500 copies. Games in hand, he began the arduous task of going door to door, selling them to shops and merchants throughout New England. By Christmas, after recouping his investment and expenses, he had sold most of the games and made close to $100 in profits. By 1888, George and his brother Charles had a healthy games business up and running. Their third brother, Edward, joined the company in 1898 and they incorporated the business as Parker Brothers shortly thereafter.

Unlike most people who found game companies, George Parker was happy to spend most of his time actually designing and evaluating new games. During this time he wrote, "There are many games on the market which, though bright and interesting in external appearance, are found dull and unentertaining when played." (Sadly, it is a fact that remains true to this day.)

Parker Brothers released several classic card games in the early 1900s. Bridge and other games played with traditional cards were seen as instruments of immorality at this time, much to the frustration of game inventors. George began working on a card game that would be fun to play, but wouldn't have the gambling associations of traditional card games. He published *Pit* in 1904, a card game that played like a traditional game but was based on trading commodities in the stock market. You can still find *Pit* selling well on shelves today. *Flinch* and *Rook* soon followed suit, so to speak, with *Rook* becoming the

65

best-selling game in the country by 1913. (Remember, kids weren't even allowed to play Go Fish.) More than 55 million *Rook* decks have been sold since 1906.

Through the twentieth century, Parker Brothers became and remained the biggest game company in the world, acquiring dozens of best-selling games along the way, including *Monopoly*, which saved the company from financial ruin during the Great Depression in 1935.

George Parker died in 1953 at the age of 86. He was a man who made his fortune playing games and brought countless hours of laughter and good memories to nearly every child in America during his lifetime.

Rook has been in print since 1906

Chapter 13

Hobby Games You Should Know

M arket leader Games Workshop correctly points out that a hobby is something people make time for, not something they do to pass the time. Indeed, for many hobby gamers getting together to play games is the focus of their social lives, a passion, and an obsession. Hobby games are great for kids and adults alike. If you talk to fans in this segment they'll tell you how *D&D* cured their shyness and taught them to read, or how *Magic* taught them to focus on a complex task and make friends. Kids who are drawn to hobby games are often exceptionally bright and looking for an intellectual challenge they don't get at school. It's not surprising that adults who play hobby games are also intellectually sophisticated. Hobby gamers are not only hungry for knowledge, they also have an insatiable appetite for game products. It's not unusual for a fan to spend hundreds of dollars a year on games.

Currently, the hobby gaming market falls into three categories, sometimes called the three pillars of the industry. They are, in order of market size, trading card games, miniatures games, and role-playing games.

Magic: the Gathering (Wizards of the Coast)

Magic blew the doors off the hobby gaming industry in a way never seen before or since. Richard Garfield, a former math professor, put the game together in 1993 for an aerospace engineer named Peter Adkison. Peter ran a small game business called Wizards of the Coast out of his garage. Incidentally, Wizards of the Coast was named after an organization in Peter's ongoing *Dungeons & Dragons* game. First released at the Milwaukee Gen Con game convention in August 1993, the game was such a runaway success that it sold out almost as soon as it hit store shelves for nearly two years. Today, even after many imitators, it sells more than $100 million a year and is stronger than ever. In fact, *Magic* presented a completely new business model and launched a whole new industry of trading card games, an industry that continues to expand to this day with annual sales close to $1 billion.

Magic comes in booster packs the same way baseball cards are packaged. Instead of sports figures, the cards have game infor- mation and fantasy-themed illustrations. Players open packs and choose which cards they wish to play with. Once players have

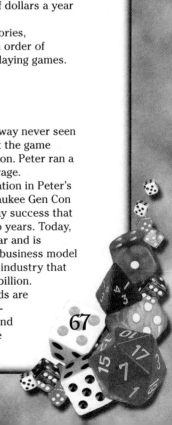

67

selected their favorite cards with which to build their decks they face off, playing cards representing magical spells and monsters until one player's point total is reduced from twenty to zero.

Magic's success is rooted in three brilliant innovations. First, it introduced the concept of game cards as collectables. With different levels of card scarcities in the packs, opening them gives players a level of excitement akin to buying a lottery ticket. Who knows whether you'll open a "rare" worth $20, or whether you'll pull out "trash rares?" Trading and collecting adds a new dimension of strategy for players trying to acquire the cards needed to assemble the perfect combination. Further, since the cards in a collection are worth money, players don't mind paying hundreds of dollars for packs since they can always sell their collections to recoup some of the costs if they decide to quit the game.

Prices on Magic cards

Secondly, the game rapidly changes over time. Cards available in 2002 are out of print and difficult to find in 2003. In fact, most of those cards will never see print again. Since Wizards releases new cards on a regular basis, even players who dedicate their lives to mastering the game constantly have to invent new strategies to deal with and exploit the latest card "technology." This is a level of strategic sophistication never before seen in a static game. The sum of all the elements that allow a player to participate in the game when he's not actually playing is known as the "metagame." Elements of *Magic's* metagame include collecting, trading, building decks, and analyzing what opponents are playing.

The third brilliant innovation was the development of the

Magic tournament

strongest organized play program in the world. The DCI (Duelist's Convocation International) is Wizards of the Coast's sanctioning organization, overseeing and managing an astounding 100,000 *Magic* tournaments per year! Here's how it works: Tournament organizers (often game store owners) advertise a tournament and provide playing space and rules adjudication. Players show up, pay the organizer an entry fee and play, most often playing for fun, but also for prizes and to improve their ratings. The organizer reports the results of each match to the DCI, which then records it in its database. Each player's lifetime record contributes to a ranking among all other players in the world. The highest rated players gain access to the invitation-only *Magic: the Gathering* Pro Tour that gives away $3 million a year in prize money. This organization far surpasses in scope the rating systems of better-known games such as Bridge or Chess. More importantly, it gives the players a sense of community that keeps them invested in the game as an important part of their social lives.

Magic owes much of its continued success to what is probably the best R&D team in the business. Imagine the challenge of designing new, interesting, uncomplicated cards when there are already over 5,600 different cards in publication. Lead designer Bill Rose, along with designers Mark Rosewater, Mike Elliott, and myself, have managed to consistently turn out around 600 new cards a year, every year. A crew of six full-time developers led by Randy Buehler, also make sure all the new cards work well in conjunction with all previously published ones.

Dungeons & Dragons (Wizards of the Coast)

Gary Gygax and Dave Arneson invented *D&D* in 1974, not suspecting it would create the role-playing games industry. After waxing in the mid-1980s and waning in the mid-1990s, *D&D* has gained tremendous ground in the past few years under the stewardship of Wizards of the Coast. The release of Third Edition *D&D* in 1999 ushered in a new age of role-playing in the hobby games industry.

Dungeons & Dragons handbooks from 1974

In the past, *D&D* has been a scapegoat for neglectful parents with absurd claims of occultism and violent behavior, although fashion has shifted most of this blame to computer games in the last 10 years. If parents ever met the crew of *D&D* designers they'd be far more worried about their kids growing up to be nerds than cultists.

The game of *D&D* is frequently misunderstood because game play is so different from traditional games familiar to most people. The game has no board or cards, only paper, pencil, dice, and rulebooks. The players aren't actually even competing to win. The only real goal of the game is to tell an interesting fantasy story and see how each player can influence the outcome. One player takes the title of the Dungeon Master. He or she dreams up a story and setting, such as "A town is being invaded by monsters and it's up to you to protect it." Each player brings a character modeled after various archetypes from fantasy fiction, such as a Wizard, Barbarian, and so forth. The DM simply imagines and describes each step of the story: "Three Minotaurs burst out of the castle door and attack you!" The players respond in turn describing how their characters deal with the situation: "I shoot an arrow!" "I run away!" Battle (and nearly everything else for that matter) is resolved with dice and extensive rules. Let's be clear: very extensive rules. Most players know, or have even memorized, the 282-page *Player's Handbook*. Dungeon Masters are expected to thoroughly know another 500 or so pages from the *Dungeon Master's Guide* and *Monster Manual*. Thousands more pages of supplements are also available for serious enthusiasts. Strangely, games typically don't really end. (At least not until players quit or move away.) Players simply leave off after a few hours and pick up the story at the next meeting again and again for months or even years. With dedicated players, a typical game might last 150 hours over the course of a year.

In 2000, Wizards of the Coast did something with *D&D* no one expected: They gave their rules away for free. Up to that point, dozens of different companies had published their own rule

Dungeons & Dragons handbooks from 2001

systems for role-playing games. That meant if you wanted to play a mystery horror game, or a mobster story, or any role-playing game that was set in another world, you had to buy it from a different company and use a different set of rules. Wizards' new d20 Open Gaming License essentially allowed anyone to publish a game with any kind of story or setting using the proprietary *D&D* rule systems that Wizards owned (these rules are called the d20 system because of their reliance on 20-sided dice). Some Wizards executives argued that they would be giving a huge boost to competitors by letting them use the best rules system in the industry. They were right, but it also turned out to be a huge benefit for players, Wizards of the Coast, and everyone else. Now that competitors could concentrate on writing interesting stories instead of rules, and players were pretty much assured of knowing the rules of any new game they bought, sales of role-playing games increased across the board, both for small publishers and for Wizards of the Coast.

In fact, thanks to the d20 license, publishing adventures for role-playing games is again one of the most robust businesses in hobby games. Although inexperienced, aspiring writers likely won't sell all that many copies, it's not difficult to self-publish, self-promote, and sell enough copies to cover your expenses and pay your way to some conventions.

Warhammer (Games Workshop)

Warhammer is the world's most successful miniatures wargame, and makes up the majority of sales in miniatures—the third pillar of the hobby games market. Miniatures games are battle simulations using anywhere from a handful to hundreds of tiny figurines. *Warhammer* figures are cast in metal and are about one-and-one-half inches high.

Warhammer hobbyists purchase the figures they want, then assemble, modify, and paint them according to their own tastes. Many of these models require hours of preparation before they can be played. Once a player has collected and prepared an army, he

Rulebooks or reference sheets are used to play Warhammer

faces off against an opponent on a large table with miniaturized terrain. Each figure has game statistics in a separate rulebook and players reference these as they roll dice to resolve battles and use measuring tapes to mark distances and move troops. Games

Gamers can paint their figures to give them a unique look

typically take a few hours to finish, depending on how many figures are involved. How many figures is that? Often dozens and dozens. It's not unusual for each side to bring fifty figures, each painted in exacting detail.

Warhammer comes in several varieties, the most successful

of which is the science fiction version called *Warhammer 40,000* (frequently abbreviated *Warhammer 40K*). *Warhammer* is another product with a strong metagame, and also has a robust organized play program. In fact for many players the metagame is more important than the game itself. For example, *Warhammer* fans typically spend far more time painting and plotting than they ever do battling.

Mage Knight (WizKids)

Mage Knight and its superhero version *HeroClix* are upstarts in the miniatures category. Conventional wisdom held that Games Workshop had an unbreakable hold on miniatures players, but *Mage Knight* came out of nowhere in November of 2000 to challenge that assumption with spectacular results.

Mage Knight figures

Mage Knight was revolutionary product due to three innovations. First, it applied the collectable trading card model to miniatures. Figures are sold randomly in sealed boxes. You never know what figures you're going to get. Second, the miniatures are plastic and come already painted, so they're much cheaper and you can start playing as soon as you buy them. *Warhammer*, on the other hand, requires players to spend about $90 each and many hours painting before they can even think about playing. The third innovation was a new type of clickable base for the figure to stand on. The base rotates like a dial, with new information about the figure becoming visible as the fighter is injured. For example, say a figure has an attack value of 10. After that figure is wounded, its attack isn't as effective, so you click the base one space to the left and a new attack value of 8 shows through the little window.

WizKids, the company that publishes *Mage Knight*, likes to tout the clickable bases as the game's most revolutionary element. It's my opinion that the clickable bases don't deserve all of the credit for its success. By far, the most important innovation was packaging the figures in randomized sealed boxes with different rarities. The act of opening the box to see which figures you get is so exciting it really becomes a big part of the game's appeal. Also, like *Magic* and *Pokémon*, it creates a secondary market so players can sell their figures and justify spending a lot of money on them.

HeroClix was WizKids' next high profile release, applying the *Mage Knight* game engine to the superhero genre. Scoring a fantastic licensing deal with both Marvel and DC Comics, WizKids released such iconic heroes as Superman, Spider-Man, Batman, and The Hulk. Released in 2002, *HeroClix* was one of the largest releases of a hobby gaming product ever, with about 3 million figures sold in the first two weeks! Since then the company has also released a fighting war machines game called *BattleTech*.

DC HeroClix "Flash," Mage Knight "Solonavi Striker,"
Mechwarrior: Dark Age "CMG"

Chapter 14

Hobby Game Companies You Should Know

Wizards of the Coast

If you've read the earlier chapters of this book you already know the story of how Richard Garfield brought *Magic: the Gathering* to Peter Adkison and stunned the game industry by creating the tremendously popular new category of trading card games.

Wizard of the Coast's main lobby

The growth of Wizards was an incredible phenomenon from a business perspective as well. Profitable within the first day of *Magic's* release, the company was flooded with both cash and consumer demand from the very beginning. Company executives, most of whom had almost no business experience, hired their friends, neighbors, and anyone else who seemed to know what they were doing. They even

75

recruited the local Camarilla, a live-action role-playing organization (people who dress up and pretend to be vampires) and went down the list, calling people to see if they wanted jobs. For years afterwards the company was dotted with black-garbed Goths who came to work daily dressed in 19th century clothing.

Because Wizards couldn't print enough *Magic* cards to meet consumer demand, retail shops got in the habit of ordering twice the number of cards they really needed,

Peter Adkison, Founder of Wizards of the Coast

hoping to get half their order filled. In 1995, the company finally had the money to print enough cards and actually filled all the orders. To their horror, half of the cards were sent back, leading to massive revenue shortfalls and unexpected layoffs. This and other lessons from the school of hard knocks slowly transformed the callow company it once was into a stable industry leader that today employs many of the best people in gaming.

Wizards acquired TSR in 1997, and with it the floundering *D&D*. Wizards also developed America's largest chain of specialty game retail stores in the late '90s. The influx of cash from *Pokémon* enabled them to secure high-profile locations in many of the nations premier shopping malls.

Acquired by Hasbro in 1998, Wizards is the biggest hobby game company in the world, doing around $250 million a year in sales. Their main business is role-playing games and trading card games, but the New Business Development team is constantly exploring opportunities to break into new categories that have a repeat purchase business model.

Unfortunately, Wizards does not accept submissions from unpublished inventors. Other important products by Wizards of the Coast include the *Harry Potter*, *Star Wars*, and *Major League Baseball*

76

trading card games.

Games Workshop

Games Workshop knows its business. While other companies have tried to branch out into new markets with mixed results, Games Workshop has adopted a strategy of doing one thing and doing it well. Their focus has never strayed from metal miniatures war games, a business that earns them around $80 million a year.

They are clearly the dominant force in the miniatures industry and have

adopted some unusual strategies to remain so. Early on, they realized not every player had the space required for a large battle layout. It was important to have a place for fans to

A wide selection of miniatures from Games Workshop

gather and promote the hobby. Their solution was to open retail shops, with 120 locations throughout the UK, 61 in mainland Europe, and 37 in North America. Their shops are small and packed with miniatures, paints, terrain, *Warhammer* books, and nothing else. The only products they sell are their own. The success of this strategy has allowed them to keep a lock on hobby gaming in England. Since they refuse to carry anyone else's products, it's quite difficult for trading cards and role-playing games to reach customers in these areas.

Executives at Games Workshop have also acknowledged that their typical consumer is fiercely loyal, but only for a few years. The model *Warhammer* player is a boy who tends to pick up the hobby around age 12 or so, until he drops it when he discovers cars and girls at about 15. With this in mind, the company's business strategy is engineered to get maximum revenue from him while they can. Models cost around $6 each (remember, you probably buy at least 50 of them) and customized paints and terrain are comparably expensive.

Games Workshop also has an unusual style of marketing. If you take a look at their magazine, store layouts, and ads, everything is focused on their current release. Unlike other companies, which support their older titles with marketing, once a new *Warhammer* series is released, it eclipses the previous ones entirely.

Another interesting fact is that GW is a publicly traded company

on the London Stock Exchange. So are Mattel and Hasbro, but GW is only one-thirtieth the size of these giants. Thus, its finances are a matter of public record for investors and it has relatively more scrutiny and less autonomy than privately owned companies of its size.

WizKids

WizKids is a company of about 50 employees located near Seattle, Washington. Veteran game designer Jordan Weisman founded WizKids in 2000 after past successes with the *Battletech* miniatures, role-playing, and computer game properties. Jordan's goal was an

A Mage Knight dragon model

audacious one: to challenge the juggernaut of Games Workshop and create a new category of collectable miniatures.

The company strategy was to design a game that eliminated the huge barrier to entry new players faced when picking up a miniatures game. Instead of forcing customers to spend hundreds of dollars on figures and countless hours painting them, their goal was to create a game that was both affordable to kids and playable as soon as the box was opened.

Mage Knight met these goals with resounding success, as evidenced by its sales of over 40 million figures in its first 14 months, an incredible achievement. WizKids followed up *Mage Knight's* success with *HeroClix*, another wildly successful game that uses similar rules for battles with superhero figurines.

TSR

TSR originally stood for Tactical Studies Rules. Although TSR as a company no longer exists, having been purchased and absorbed into Wizards of the Coast in 1997, it was undeniably one of the most important game companies in the business for 25 years. Grown from a tiny basement operation into a 400-person company in a few short years, the company spent so much time rushing to meet consumer demand that they sometimes ignored things that other companies took for granted, like facilities. Early TSR employee Jeff Grubb recalls a time in 1982 when the office was located in a condemned hotel. People had to move to one side of the room since the entire building would lean to one side when enough people came to the meeting. TSR eventually moved to modern facilities, but demand didn't let up. At the peak of *D&D's* popularity in the early 1980s, TSR was even getting *D&D* into the mass market distribution channels.

Despite TSR's massive financial success with *D&D*, its executive management was plagued with infighting and backstabbing. Dave Arneson had already left the company and Gary Gygax was forced out as well in 1986. To make matters worse, the company branched into a number of unprofitable ventures (including a needlecraft business) that essentially squandered *D&D's* profits. With Gary gone, a new president took the helm, and despite having no experience in the gaming industry, seemed to be leading the company to recovery. That is, until 1994 when *Magic: the Gathering* rocked the gaming world and TSR made a number of disastrous strategic decisions in response.

Scrambling to compete with the trading card collecting frenzy, TSR developed a collectible dice game called *Dragon Dice*. Initial response was excellent. Although the cost of manufacturing was outrageous, it seemed TSR had a serious hit on its hands. Just like trading cards, product was flying off the shelf and the company couldn't keep pace with demand. Unlike trading cards, the market dried up after only a year. In its exuberance to be part of the collectible phenomenon, TSR had just ordered a new production run of dice that was bigger than all the previous sales combined. Shiploads of dice

Dragon Dice

were on their way towards America with no one wanting to buy them. It was a financial disaster that basically ensured the company's bankruptcy.

Luckily, the man responsible for the collecting phenomenon that destroyed TSR also turned out to be its savior. Peter Adkison, founder of Wizards of the Coast, was a lifelong *D&D* player with a passion for the game that wouldn't allow him to see it die. He negotiated the sale of the crippled TSR to Wizards

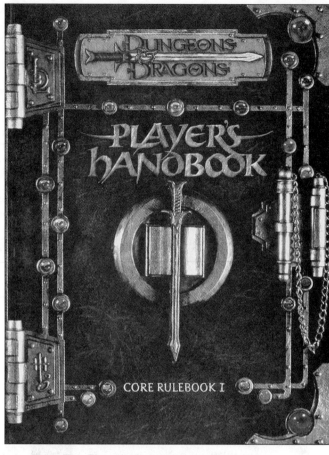

The Player's Handbook for 3rd Edition
Dungeons & Dragons

and moved the company to Wizards' Seattle headquarters in 1997. It was clear to many that Peter loved *D&D* so much he would have done nearly anything to save it.

It was the right decision. Today, sales of *D&D* products are over $15 million a year and role-playing games are a robust part of the hobby gaming industry.

INSIDER'S VIEW—INVENTOR: MIKE FITZGERALD

Mike Fitzgerald has designed 14 published games to date, including *Mystery Rummy*, *Wyvern*, and *Wyatt Earp*. His games have sold well in nearly every distribution channel from the mass market to Germany to the hobby game industry, a feat equaled by few designers.

Mike Fitzgerald

A lifelong game enthusiast, Mike achieved a Master rating in chess at an early age and had a tremendous breadth of experience in the kinds of games he played. With his energetic personality and persistent attitude, Mike found success in his day job as a radio deejay in New York City. In fact, he broke into the radio industry by going into a studio and refusing to leave the lobby until they gave in and listened to his demo tape 6 hours later. Cursed with an inability to stop thinking about new ideas, Mike took a similarly straightforward approach to getting involved in the game industry. He called up his favorite game company, Avalon Hill, and asked if they needed anyone to playtest new games. It turned out

that they did, and weren't about to turn down some free brain power. They began sending him prototypes of unpublished games. Mike got a play group together and dug into them with gusto. He and his group played these unfinished products on a regular basis, discussing problems and possible improvements along the way. Though not aware of it at the time, this experience helped him learn to think like a game designer, preparing him for an opportunity that would change his life.

Fast forward to New York City, Toy Fair, 1994. Toy Fair is an industry-only trade show not open to the general public. Ever resourceful, Mike recalls, "Because of my radio job I was able to get a press pass for the show. I really wasn't looking for work in games. I was mostly just interested in seeing the new releases and checking out all the cool stuff going on." Little did he know he was about to experience a turning point in his career. The show was abuzz with the news of *Magic: the Gathering*. Like many hardcore gamers, Mike had been quickly drawn in by *Magic's* strategic depth. He happened to be walking by with a handful of cards when Stuart Kaplan of U.S. Games stopped to ask him about them.

Stuart asked, "We've been thinking about doing a game like *Magic*. Do you know anyone who could design one?" Without thinking, Mike blurted out "Sure … I could." Stuart mentioned that they had an artist with a bunch of good dragon illustrations so they were interested in a dragon-themed game. "No problem," Mike replied, "I'll have something for you in a month." Stuart thought that sounded reasonable and they made a deal on the spot.

Unfortunately Mike had never designed a game for publication before. Rising to the challenge, Mike was actually able to have a bare-bones design ready in a month, but it took four or five more months for him to flesh it out to publication quality. The result was *Wyvern*, a dragon-themed trading card game that was one of the first of many trading card games to hit the market on the heels of *Magic*. Hungry for new products in the fledgling trading card industry, distributors loved the game and bought it as fast as it could be printed. Though it was ultimately overprinted, *Wyvern's* success catapulted Mike into the ranks of sought-after game designers and opened many doors for his submissions to other companies.

Mike bought a house with *Wyvern's* first royalty check.

Chapter 15

American Specialty Games And Companies You Should Know

"American specialty games" is sort of a catchall category for American games that aren't mass market or hobby games. It includes games targeted to a certain segment, such as strategy board games, sports simulations, "How to Host a Mystery" games, and so forth. Generally, you should expect small print runs from small publishers, but on the bright side it's definitely the easiest category for newcomers to get started.

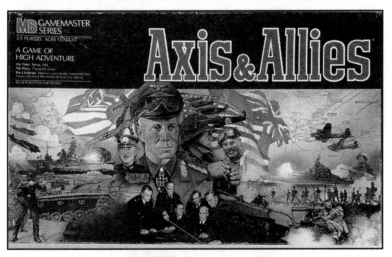

Milton Bradley's Axis & Allies

Avalon Hill and Axis & Allies

Avalon Hill was the closest thing to a hobby game company before the hobby game industry really existed. It has a long and well-respected history and has published countless small titles over the years, often loaded with hundreds of plastic figures and cardboard

83

chits. Avalon Hill is best known for its historical strategic warfare games, the best known of which is the World War II game *Axis & Allies*, which has sold over a million units.

Today Avalon Hill is part of Wizards of the Coast after being purchased by Hasbro. Other Avalon Hill titles worth checking out are *Cosmic Encounter*, *Risk 2210*, *Acquire*, *Diplomacy*, and *Battle Cry*.

Out of the Box and Apples to Apples

Out of the Box has managed to make fans of families and casual gamers with a distinct style of party game. The company's products are simple enough for the mass market consumer, but have a level of depth, interaction, and play value that most mass market games can't capture. Despite not being carried by most of the mass market retailers, the company does tremendous volume, mostly through word of mouth recommendations from its loyal fans. The company's biggest hit, *Apples to Apples* is a perennial bestseller and winner of 11 national awards. For more information on Out of the Box, check out the interview with company president Mark Osterhaus on page 86.

Mayfair

A large part of Mayfair's business is in marketing German games in the U.S. As such, many of its most important products are strategy board games. Some of its best-known titles include the American versions of *Settlers of Catan*, the *18XX train series*, *Knizia's Modern Art*, *Quo Vadis*, and *Tigris & Euphrates*. Mayfair also does some business in assorted role-playing and other hobby games and accessories.

Variations of The Settlers of Catan

Rio Grande

Rio Grande is another company specializing in German-style, or "designer" games. They have the U.S. rights to publish *Carcassone*, *Bohnanza*, *Lost Cities*, *Wyatt Earp*, *Medici*, *Torres*, *Elfenland*, *Mississippi Queen*, *Java*, and *Tikal*. Rio Grande lists some interesting links to U.S. gaming groups and German game companies on their Web site at http://www.riograndegames.com/

Fossil, a Rio Grande Game

Decipher and How to Host a Murder

Decipher is a major player in both the hobby gaming industry, with its *Lord of the Rings Trading Card Game*, and in the specialty market with the *How to Host a Mystery* series, among other games.

How to Host a Murder is the first "LARP" (an acronym for "Live Action Role-playing"). Everyone else calls this play-acting. The game is really an instruction manual for a dinner party in which everyone plays the role of a murder suspect. Players are encouraged to wear costumes and speak in character as they arrive for dinner at the host's residence. Booklets are handed to each guest to provide guidance and help players ask each other questions to elicit clues. Near the end, everyone guesses whom the guilty one is then reads the resolution to see if they were right. Themes are often humorous and much of the fun comes from watching friends overacting the melodramatic parts.

INSIDER'S VIEW— PUBLISHER: OUT OF THE BOX

O ut of the Box is an inspiring success story that's pretty unusual. It's a great example of what can happen when company leaders begin with a clear objective and consumer in mind and manage their products well. The company will sell about half a million units a year in 2002, with about 20 games in its current product line—all this from a company that's less than 5 years old.

I met with CEO Mark Osterhaus to talk about how the company manages to thrive in a marketplace dominated by big competitors.

Brian: "Tell me about your company."

Mark: "It was my idea to start a game company. I had a good background in marketing—I worked for software firms and Trek bicycles among others. After being in the business world for 20 years I decided I was tired of working for someone else.

Mark Osterhaus

Of course I was a lifelong gamer. I realized I needed help, so I started looking up people I knew that I'd worked with over the years. I brought in three other people I trusted as employees and investors. We really are a bootstrap company. We had no other

86

investors besides the four of us who put it together. Al Waller was a guy I worked with in the software business in the Eighties. He wasn't from the game industry, but he really knew how to build distribution networks. Building up relationships with distribution partners and retailers was really key to our success and that was his strength. Kathleen Quinn-Kinney was a graphic designer who understood how to do prepress and preproduction work, so she was a great partner. The third person was John Kovalic, an up-and-coming cartoonist whose art was essential in our products. We started the company in 1998.

"From there, our vision was to become the next great American game company. That sounds kind of strange, but let me explain the philosophy behind that. Games were a popular entertainment choice in the early part of the century all the way through the Seventies. But since the early Eighties games have been on the decline. Computer games, among other things that compete for people's spare time and dollars, started pulling younger people away. Hasbro bought all the main companies in the industry—Parker Brothers, Milton Bradley, Selchow & Righter. The problem is Hasbro doesn't have the ability to launch innovative new products. They don't have the patience to let a new concept take off. It takes time to create a big hit and they want to see big dollars immediately. So none of the major companies have the ability to respond to people's changing needs.

"Look at Hasbro's promotion called 'Family Game Night.' It tells people they should set aside time one night a week to play games. What they're doing is asking people to change their lifestyles to fit Hasbro's products. What we want to do is create products that fit peoples' lifestyles. But that means you have to redesign the game engine."

Brian: "So what are the elements that make your games different?"

Mark: "There has to be simultaneous play or something similar that keeps everyone involved every turn. We don't want anyone sitting around doing nothing. The learning threshold has to be almost zero. The game cycle [how long it takes to play] has to be right. It should fit the player's attention span and not take too long to play. The most important element is the total fun factor. You can have a good game that's not fun. Maybe it meets all the right points and plays well, but do you want to play it again?"

Brian: "How many game concepts do you look at each year?"

Mark: "About five to ten a week. I only look at proposals from e-mail."

Brian: "How long does it take to get a product from the idea stage to the stores?"

Mark: "Six to nine months. Once we know we want to do a game we can get it out very quickly."

87

Brian: "What are the most common mistakes you see inventors make?"

Mark: [rolling eyes] "Oh man. Overestimating the value of their idea. Their expectations for sales are way too high. I see proposals constantly that use words like 'one million' or 'the next *Trivial Pursuit*' or 'millionaires.' It just shows they don't know what it takes to sell that many games. If you're going to pull a number out of the air, why not say 'two million,' or 'eight and a half million?' When they write stuff like that what they're really saying is 'I don't like my job. I wish I could be rich.'

"Another problem is new inventors are too suspicious. I've seen people spend tens of thousands of dollars patenting their game and getting lawyers for protection, but I've never seen a legitimate case of idea theft by a game company. Ask around. It's a waste of money and effort. Sometimes I even get submissions sent by the inventor's lawyers. It just signals that the inventor is naïve."

Brian: "What are some other mistakes you see inventors make?"

Mark: "The games just aren't original. They're just too willing to follow the configuration of another game. If I can look at something and say 'that's based on *Monopoly*' I'm already not interested. They're too willing to do variations on a theme. What else? Too many trivia games. Seems like everyone wants to invent a trivia game and no one wants to play them.

"One thing I see all the time is too much clutter in a game. They tend to overbuild their designs. It just gets in the way of the fun parts."

Brian: "Is there any advice you would give to new inventors?"

Mark: "Test your game with people you don't know. Don't rely on family and friends to be honest critics. I also really advise against getting investors [and publishing the game yourself]. Get a publisher instead. You absolutely need business experience if you're going to try to do it yourself. Imagine blowing all your money and waking up one morning with a warehouse full of games you don't know what to do with. Your only hope is to borrow even more money and risk losing that too. It really happens, and you don't want to be in that spot."

Chapter 16

European Games, Companies, And An Award You Should Know

It's an interesting cultural difference that games are quite a bit more popular in Europe, and especially Germany, than they are in North America. Also unlike the U.S. market, where there's a stark contrast between the huge mass market publishers and the small independent publishers, Europe has a wide array of publisher sizes including the mid-sized companies the U.S. lacks. Another interesting difference is that Europeans generally like their games to be highly strategic and thoughtful. Games that sell in the hundreds of thousands in Europe often sell less than ten thousand in North America because Americans find them too complex. German publishers can certainly be an attractive market if your game is focused on strategy. In fact, there's an effort to rename what Americans call "German games" to "designer games," since they're custom-designed for game

A wide selection of german board games

89

enthusiasts.

Unlike American games, designer games display the game designer's name as boldly as books display their authors. Designer name recognition can actually help drive sales. If you want to look up some of the most well-known European games in the market, check out designs by Klaus Teuber, Wolfgang Kramer, and of course, the inexhaustible Reiner Knizia.

Ravensberger

Ravensberger is Germany's largest game company with around 2,000 employees and sales of about $300 million a year, although a significant portion of its revenue comes from puzzles, toys, TV production, and book publishing.

Tikal

Ravensberger has an astounding 850 game titles.

Tikal, by Wolfgang Kramer and Michael Kiesling, is one of Ravensberger's recent noteworthy games. The 1999 Spiel Des Jahres (German Game of the Year) winner, *Tikal* puts players in the roles of expedition leaders uncovering lost Mayan ruins in the jungles of Guatemala. Players search for hidden temples and treasures, turning over tiles to reveal surprises as they explore the jungle. Each player has a certain number of action points to spend doing things like placing workers, exploring temples, and setting up camps. When players turn over a volcano tile, the turn ends and scores are added up.

Alea

Alea is a mid-sized German company that publishes a modest number of strategy board game titles. One of Alea's notable titles is Riener

RA

Knizia's ancient Egyptian-themed *RA*. Players start with a fixed amount of bidding chips, each with different values. The goal is to outbid the opponents in order to collect tiles worth the most points. The tiles are worth different amounts of points depending on what combinations of them each player collects.

Strategy board games that focus on bidding are fairly popular in Germany, but relatively unknown in the United States. You may also notice that Germany has very few games that rely on the American model of "roll the dice and move the token around the board." Instead, the games deal with building cities and empires, exploration, and trading. Notably absent are games that deal with war.

Kosmos

Kosmos is another top publisher in Germany. Its claim to fame is the most popular German game of the past two decades, Klaus Teuber's *Settlers of Catan*. *Settlers*, or "Siedler" as it's known in Germany, won the Spiel des Jahres in 1995. Today it has sold more than a million copies with many expansions and variants. It's an unusual example of a German game that made the leap to North America and actually enjoyed strong sales which continue to this day. In *Settlers*, players represent fledgling civilizations colonizing an island. The board consists of hexagonal tiles that are randomly assembled at the beginning of the game so the board is different

The Settlers of Catan

each time you play. Players draw resources from whichever tiles they're touching and attempt to build roads and expand their civilizations. It's an elegant combination of strategy, politics, and luck that strikes a chord with many people.

Hans Im Glück

Hans Im Glück is a relative newcomer to the top tier German publisher list, but it has recently moved up in the world with the success of its Spiel des Jahres winner *Carcassonne* by Klaus-Jurgen Wrede. *Carcassonne* is an interesting, quick-playing game where players lay down tiles to build the roads and cities of the medieval French countryside. Each turn a player draws a tile, places it somewhere next to another tile, and may lay claim to an empty road, city, field, or building. Surprisingly easy to learn, it's a good example of a wildly

Carcassonne

successful game that avoids the typical move-pieces-on-a-board model that limits many designers' thinking.

Amigo

Rounding out the list of top German publishers is Amigo, with its 1998 hit *Elfenland* by Alan Moon. In *Elfenland*, players represent elves racing to traverse a fairytale continent and be the first to collect an entire set of tokens. Each turn players alternate playing tiles which represent modes of transportation along various paths. The strategy is in planning your

Elfenland

route and using opponents' modes of transportation in conjunction with your own. You might have to ride a pig, a boat, and a dragon all in one turn to get to your destination.

92

Spiel Des Jahres

Spiel Des Jahres (German for "Game of the Year") is the most coveted game award in Europe. Each year a committee of professionals selects a single family game and a single children's game as the best ones published that year. The award carries so much value with German consumers that the winning game is virtually assured of sales in the half-million copies range, or even higher. That means royalties near $500,000 for those keeping track at home. Designers who win Spiel Des Jahres are celebrated as the hottest in the industry and are almost assured of publishers clamoring to take their next designs. Needless to say, you should probably be familiar with the winners of the last several years if you want to discuss German games.

Recent Spiel Des Jahres Family Game Winners (and publishers)

2002 *Villa Piletti* (Zoch)
2001 *Carcassonne* (Hans im Glück)
2000 *Torres* (Ravensberger)
1999 *Tikal* (Ravensberger)
1998 *Elfenland* (Amigo)
1997 *Mississippi Queen* (Goldsieber)
1996 *El Grande* (Ravensberger)
1995 *Die Siedler von Catan* [Settlers of Catan] (Kosmos)
1994 *Manhattan* (Hans im Glück)
1993 *Bluff* (FX Schmid)

INSIDER'S VIEW—
INVENTOR: ALAN MOON

Alan Moon is one of the industry's most highly regarded designers, with around 45 published games in North America and Europe. His game *Elfenland* won Europe's highest game award, Spiel des Jahres, in 1998. In December of 2000 he was making enough royalties to quit his day job and devote himself to inventing and selling games full time. His success rate in placing games with publishers is now among the highest in the industry. Though he's an American, most of his current game designs are aimed at German publishers.

Alan Moon

Brian: "How did you first get involved in the game business?"

Alan: "I've always been involved with games one way or another. I started out writing articles for the *General* [Avalon Hill's former game magazine] in 1976. I did a good enough job that I was hired as the editor. At some point I realized it was too much work to be an editor and started working on games. Avalon Hill had a storeroom with a big pile of homemade games in boxes. I grabbed [head of the company] Don Greenwood and asked him 'what's this?' It turned out to be a pile of prototypes inventors had sent to Avalon Hill, but nobody had evaluated. I started going through them, selected a few, and that's how I got to be involved in

94

putting out new games."

Brian: "What was the first game you got published?"

Alan: "It was a card game called *Black Spy*, a hearts variant. I worked for the company and was publishing games so it wasn't hard to get one of mine into the product line."

Brian: "What drew you to the European market?"

Alan: "After I moved on from Avalon Hill I worked at Parker Brothers from 1983 to 1984. After that I worked as a consultant and during that time I got into German games. German games are just more interesting. There's more going on compared to American games—which are mostly simple variations on a couple of themes. If you have an interesting design your chances are just better over there. They put out so many new games that there's more demand."

Brian: "Tell me about how you invented *Elfenland*."

Alan: "It actually started out as a train game called *Thunder on the Tracks*. During playtesting I found that I needed two different types of air transportation. I dropped the train theme for a fantasy one so I could introduce dragons and magic clouds. I called the game *Elfenroads* and it was published in '92. Several years later I was talking with [German game publisher] Amigo, and they said they would be interested in a simpler version. I reworked the game and came up with *Elfenland*, which came out in '98. There was excitement for *Elfenland* from its debut at the Nurenburg Toy Show. It was a favorite for Spiel des Jahres from the beginning, which it won that year. Since then, it's sold 600,000 copies."

Brian: "Where do you start when inventing a new game?"

Alan: "Let's see. A new game can come from playing a bad game with a good idea at its center. Or from playing a game I like and can maybe take in a different direction. Or it can start with a theme. Or with components. Or with a game play mechanic I like. I believe most games come from other games."

Brian: "What are some lessons you've learned about game design?"

Alan: "You need to know your strengths. My strength is that after I've got an initial idea I'm good at making a game out of it. I've found that it's much more efficient to have a partner you can collaborate with on a game. Aaron [Weisblum] has been a good partner since we complement each other's strengths."

95

Brian: "How many of the games you invent actually get published?"

Alan: "Hm. In the past 2 or 3 years I've pitched about 35 games. Of those I have sold 14 so far. About 15 I am still pitching and will probably get sold, and 6 of them I have given up on. But keep in mind that I work on a number of games that I give up on before I pitch. I'd say about 60% of the ideas I work on get to the point where I'll show it to a publisher."

Brian: "What are some of the most important lessons new inventors need to learn?"

Alan: "Almost always new designers are too attached to their babies. You have to give up control. If they want it changed you have to change it. Sometimes companies change the game and there's nothing you can do about it. You have to be OK with that. I did a game where the publisher changed some elements at the last minute and screwed up the whole play balance. It's frustrating. But sometimes they make them better."

SECTION FOUR

SELF PUBLISHING

Chapter 17

What Am I Getting Into?

Most of this book assumes that once you design and develop your game you'll go looking for a publisher to manufacture and distribute it, but of course this isn't the only way to make your game happen. Many successful inventors take the whole business into their own hands and decide to self-publish.

Self-publishing can be tremendously rewarding or a path to aggravation and bankruptcy. This section is less of a step-by-step instruction manual and more of an overview of how it works. It can be a dangerous road. If you decide to take this option you should know what you're getting into.

Why would I want to self-publish?

When you self-publish you and your investors get to keep 100% of the profits. If you license a game to a publisher for 5% royalties and it sells a million dollars' worth, you would make about $50,000. On the other hand, if you publish the same game yourself and manage to sell a million dollars worth, it might be possible to keep as much as $450,000. (Please keep in mind that this is extremely difficult.)

When you self-publish you get to keep control of your idea. When you license to a publisher, unless you negotiate a remarkable contract, they will have the ability to change the artwork, gameplay, mood, theme, and anything else they feel like changing. Further, they may not even have to publish it if they change their minds.

One inventor I know licensed the science fiction game he'd been working on for three years to a medium-sized publisher in 1997. The company assigned the game to a marketing manager who loved the game and who frequently consulted the inventor on decisions about artwork. They felt the artwork was so important they even decided to delay the printing until the artist they wanted became available. Suddenly, just as the game was ready to go into production in late 1998, the publishing company assigned that marketing manager to another game that needed emergency help. The sci-fi game fell in the lap of a less competent manager who didn't even like it. In fact, besides essentially ignoring the inventor, the new guy kept finding reasons to delay the game even further. By early 2000 my friend gave up in frustration—another company had put out a similar sci-fi game with great success. It would have been difficult for his product to compete with it. Imagine how painful it was to watch five years of hopes wither and die when victory seemed so close. If you self-publish at least you'll have control of your product.

Self-publishing could actually end up being your only option for getting in print. That's not necessarily a bad thing. If your game is especially innovative you will almost certainly have trouble

98

selling it to a big company. Big companies see themselves as the experts, but if you look at history the huge, revolutionary products that created new categories all came from small startup companies. *Trivial Pursuit*, *Dungeons & Dragons*, *Uno*, *Pente*, and *Pictionary* were all too revolutionary for established publishers to recognize them for what they were.

In fact, self-publishing can be a ticket into the big leagues. Time and time again successful games, including even *Monopoly*, have gone through the following cycle:

1. The game is rejected by the experts at the big companies.
2. The inventor gets enough money together to publish it himself.
3. The game starts selling well.
4. The big publishers come knocking on the inventor's door asking if they can have it.
5. (Optional step—only happens with toughest inventors) The inventor negotiates triple the price he would have gotten if the experts had taken it in the first place.

I don't mean to knock the experts here. I've been in that role myself quite often. Big companies are counting on their experts' ability to consistently pick winners in a very risky hit-or-miss-driven industry. Often times it's the right decision for them to take a "wait and see" position with a game they're not sure about. Self-publishing can be a good way to use this fact to your advantage. When 10,000 copies fly off the shelves with very little marketing, they can't help imagining how many they could sell with the right advertising and promotions.

Why wouldn't I want to self-publish?

When you self-publish you're creating a startup business. If your game is successful then running the business will likely eat up 40, 50, 60, or even more hours of your week. If it's not successful you could end up in a lot of debt. If you self-publish you need to be ready to dedicate the main part of your life to the business should orders start pouring in. If you have important commitments like kids or a job you need to figure out ways to cope with the many demands on your time.

Apart from time commitments, running a business takes skills many people don't have. Do you know how to raise money, find reliable vendors, printers, and artists, manage employees, and do promotions? You'll need to find a place to store all the games once they're printed. And you yourself will be the person calling distributors, retailers, and even customers in order to sell them.

Perhaps the most compelling reason not to self-publish is that it's your money at risk. If your game isn't successful, say goodbye to your bank account, and likely those of your family and friends. Unless you're independently wealthy, this is a very serious consideration.

In early 2002, a businessman delivered a crisp, professional submission package to Wizards of the Coast. It came complete with a finished set of over one hundred illustrated cards, a public relations packet detailing the promotions they had run at San Diego ComiCon, and a "learn to play" CD-ROM. I estimate this gentleman had invested something approaching fifty thousand dollars into self-publishing the product. Our R&D team read the rules and saw at once that the game was yet another embarrassingly bad copy of *Pokémon*. The next day he called me up, eager to hear whether or not we wanted to license it. "Have you ever played *Pokémon*?" I asked. "No," he replied, "I just run the company. I'm more of a business guy. I have experts that I rely on for the actual game." I winced. "There's a serious problem with this game," I said. "It's directly copied from *Pokémon*." "That can't be," he said, puzzled. "My designers made it totally different from anything else. My lead designer is ranked 25th in the World Gamers, so he should know." There's no such thing as the World Gamers. This was getting ugly. "I think your designers aren't being honest with you. They copied this game from *Pokémon*, and not only are we declining to publish it, I believe you would run into legal trouble if you tried to publish it elsewhere." The silence on the other end was deafening. I imagined the blood draining from his face as he said, "You sure?" "I'm very sorry but I think you've been misled," was all I could say.

A Pokémon Theme Deck (Misty)

Chapter 18

Before You Print

Market Research

That cheery story should convince you how important it is to do some homework on your game before you start. You absolutely need to make sure you have a game that's going to sell. Step one is to find out what kind of consumers you are shooting for and what other options are already available to them. A simple place to begin is a local game store. Check out the shelves and see if there's anything like your idea already out there. Read the boxes and play them if you can. You need to figure out what's going to make your product different enough to make people reach for their wallets.

A friendly game store owner or employee can be your best friend. Look for someone who knows a lot about the products in the store—not only can she tell you what sells the best and why, she might also know people who would be interested in playtesting. Store owners are an enormously underused resource in the inventing community. Listen to their opinions on your game idea. They have more contact with the consumer than anyone else.

I went to a game store in the mall last December and asked the clerk if he had a recommendation. He led me to a display and presented a game that cost $40. "What else do you have?" I asked. He went on to show me one that cost $28, then another one for $20, then another that was only $12. The clerk knew that I probably had a price in mind for a gift item and the actual game mattered less than finding one with the right price. The lesson is that your game doesn't need to distinguish itself on gameplay or theme alone. There are lots of other ways to carve out a niche for it, including price.

If you want a chance of convincing distributors and retailers to buy your game, you need to have a certain type of person in mind when you design it. Ideally a retailer will be able to look at it and say to himself, "Hey this is perfect for all those eight-year-old wrestling fans that are always coming into my store." This is called your consumer segment. It's true that you don't want to make your segment too narrow, but a far more common mistake is to create a game aimed at "everyone." You are much better off inventing a game that motorcycle racing fans adore rather than a game everybody kind of likes.

Vendors

Once you know what your game is going to be about, who it's for, and roughly how much it will sell for, it's time to look at how much it will cost to manufacture. The folks that print the components, manufacture the pieces, and assemble the boxes are

101

collectively known as vendors. There are two ways to handle vendors.

The first way is to get a different vendor for each part of the project—one for the box, one for the pieces, one for assembly—and so forth. Each one delivers his parts to you and you take them to the next site until everything is put together. This choice is cheaper for you, but far more labor-intensive. You also run the risk of mistakes. One first-time self-publisher ordered a board 10 inches wide and a box 10 inches wide only to later discover the board needs to be smaller than the box if it's going to fit inside. There's no getting your money back if you make a mistake like that. Ouch.

The second option with vendors is to find one that will manufacture the whole game for you start to finish. This is the safest, easiest, and of course, most expensive option, but it's the one I recommend to people who want to keep their day jobs. The time and effort you save in this step is far better spent working on promotions. This option usually requires you to print 5,000 or more copies at a time.

In either case, you'll have to give the vendors specifications on a zillion little details about your game. How many colors on the box and rules? What size is each part? What quality and thickness of paper stock? What kind of glue will hold it together? Do you want the rulebook printed both sides? Stapled or folded? Once you get all these details figured out they'll ask you how many copies you want. Just like doughnuts, the price per unit goes down the more you buy. If you're not roling in cash try to get a price quote for 1,000, 5,000, and 10,000 games to start with. You'll want to get quotes from a couple of different vendors just to compare and see which one makes you the most comfortable.

There are a number of places to start looking for vendors. An obvious one is the Yellow Pages or an Internet search. Even if those two sources don't turn up any promising names, you can often call other self-publishers and ask for recommendations. Your vendor is usually going to want half his payment when he takes the job and the other half when he delivers the finished goods.

Artists

Artists aren't always the same as graphic designers. Artists provide illustrations intended to engage and fascinate the consumer—they paint the pretty dinosaurs. Graphic designers specialize in creating layouts intended to present information—they're the ones who make the backs of the cards and title logo.

One of the most important considerations for the game is what the box or cover looks like. In his excellent book, *Game Plan*, Steve Peek of University Games describes the "ritual test" consumers go through when a game grabs their attention. First the consumer picks up the box and reads the top. If your artist did his job, she turns it over and skims the headlines and pictures on the back. If the material there keeps her interested, she turns the box over to find the price sticker. With all this information in mind, she unconsciously weighs the box with her hands to see if it feels like it's worth the price. The material on the outside of the box is critically important to making the game sell. In some cases, what's on the outside of the box can even be more important than what's inside, especially when the game is unusual.

Finding an artist is going to be a lot like finding vendors. Start with a broad Internet or Yellow Pages search. Each time you contact someone, ask if they can recommend a freelance artist. You can also look at a published product you like and find out who that company used.

Here's an insider's tip: With my first few projects I didn't have much money for art so I called the local art college (The Art Institute of Seattle). It turns out they have a career placement office that's happy to recommend freelance jobs to talented students looking to build their portfolios. Students e-mailed me samples of their work until I found a couple of artists I liked. I got near-professional quality artwork for several projects at about a tenth the price it would have cost elsewhere. For example, I commissioned a batch of 20 pen-and-ink space alien illustrations for $250. The main drawback to this tactic is that students can be unreliable compared to professionals, sometimes not delivering on time or to specifications.

When you hire an artist you need a contract specifying who owns the artwork. It should specify that you own all the graphics in the game unless you want to end up paying royalties. In general, it's a good idea to get releases covering any design work done by other people.

Pricing & Budgeting

A good rule of thumb is that a consumer will have to pay about seven or eight times what it costs you to manufacture each game. For example, if the vendor charges you $2.50 to manufacture a game, you'll be able to sell it to a distributor for about $6. The distributor will sell it to a retailer for about $9.50, and the retailer will sell it for $20. (If you skip the distributor and go right to the store you'll still be able to sell it for about $9, but you'll be able to sell a lot fewer of them.) You want to keep this rule in mind when you get cost estimates from your vendors. If your game costs $7 per game to manufacture, you may need to rethink some components.

Say your game costs $3.00 to manufacture if you're running 5,000 copies. That's $15,000 for manufacturing. Artwork and graphic design might cost $3,500. Add another $2,000 for shipping, plus a tiny $4,000 promotions budget to get you to a couple of conventions and you get a total cost of $24,500.

Can you raise that much cash? If not, you'll need to bring down costs somewhere. Can you sell that many copies? The more homework you did on market demands the easier this part will be. Still, it's not uncommon for a self-publisher to end up visiting stores one by one and selling a few games at a time. Games sometimes take a few years of promotions before they really take off. In fact, *Pictionary* and *Trivial Pursuit* each took about three years of relentless marketing until they became the runaway successes we know and love.

At this stage you should also be able to figure out how much money you stand to make with the game. In our hypothetical example if you sell all 5,000 copies to distributors at $6.50 each, that's $32,500 in revenue. Subtract $24,500 in expenses and you have a best-case scenario of $8,000 to put in your pocket.

Financing

It takes money to make money. Now that you know how much you need to spend and how much revenue your first print run could

103

generate, it's time to raise that cash. Here are your basic options.

Friends and family are a logical place to start. They believe in your ability and want to see you succeed. It's perfectly fine to enlist them as investors in your project as long as you make it very clear what the risks are. You absolutely need them to understand that in this kind of a business if someone forgets to make sure the box is bigger than the board, they will lose everything they put in. If they can't afford to take this kind of risk with their money, you shouldn't risk damaging your relationship by bringing them in. The other downside is that unless you have rich relatives this option usually won't bring in all that much money.

Bank loans are another place you can try. Depending on the level of debt you're able to assume, a loan can take care of some or all of the cash you're trying to raise. If you've got a strong credit rating or can borrow against your home equity you might be able to get a personal line of credit with no questions asked. Otherwise you may need to take out a small business loan, which requires that you demonstrate a plan for what you intend to do with the money they're loaning you.

Investors are another source you can turn to for cash. Look into local organizations of startup companies and you'll find a network of wealthy individuals who are interested in getting in on the ground floor of new business ventures. Taking on investors means you'll give up full ownership of the company and you'll have to include them when making important decisions. It also means you'll have to put together a complete business plan detailing your financial goals, budget, timeline, sales plans, marketing and promotion efforts, and distribution channels. It's probably a good idea to put together a business plan like this anyway, just for your own use. A game company is a tough sell to these kinds of investors, but it seems to go in and out of fashion. It's quite possible you can swing it if the timing is right.

WizKids' Founder Jordan Weisman points out, "There's always risk when you're starting out. Remember that there are people willing to take that financial risk for you if they become passionate about your product."

Salesmanship is one of the most important skills a game inventor can have. Regardless of whether you self-publish or sell to a publisher, you'll need to get other people excited about your product. In this case, you'll have to start by selling people on the idea that your game could make a lot of money. If you do this well, you have a good chance of getting investors, friends, and loan officers interested. Later on you can use those freshly sharpened sales skills on distributors, retailers, and customers.

Whichever options you pick to raise money, I recommend you visit your local branch of the Small Business Administration (SBA). They can help you find other ways of raising money as well as helping with innumerable details such as taxes, hiring help, and getting a business license. One of the best things you can do is make an appointment with an SBA counselor who can make sure you aren't leaving out any critical parts of your business plan.

Volunteers

In the late 1980s Jonathan Tweet and Mark Rein-Hagen, fresh out of college, decided going into business looked better than getting a job, and went about publishing a roleplaying game called

Ars Magica. Since they were operating on essentially no money, they worked hard to recruit their friends and local gamers to work on the game for free. Many hobby gamers are exited about the opportunity to get their names in the credits of a published game. Using this to their advantage, the pair got dozens of hours of editing, writing, and playtesting for free. *Ars Magica* passed through many companies over the years, but is still in print today. More importantly, it laid the groundwork for the pair to become two of the most successful roleplaying game designers in the business.

Mark went on to found the well-known roleplaying game company White Wolf, while Jonathan went to Wizards of the Coast, where he became lead designer of *D&D 3rd Edition*.

Former NASA scientists Kristin and Andrew Looney built their game company Looney Labs from scratch, operating on very little money. Early on, they learned their marketing lessons the hard way. Today, almost all of their sales come from grassroots marketing efforts. After talking to numerous companies and retailers, they learned how to build a demo program and formed a solid base of fans for their award-winning games like *Fluxx*, *Chrononauts*, and *Icehouse*. Kristin relates, "Most of our experience is with direct-to-consumer guerilla marketing. We built a demo program by letting fans sign up as 'Mad Lab Rabbits.' Their job is to hang out in game stores and demonstrate products to other customers. In return, we send them special items you can't get anywhere else." Their program is administered through their Web site: www.looneylabs.com.

Chapter 19

After You Print

Promotions

If you don't have a pile of money for advertising, most of your sales are going to come from word of mouth. Don't underestimate it as a marketing strategy. When someone you know recommends a great product, it's infinitely more compelling than seeing an ad. Some of the most effective word of mouth comes from game store employees who recommend your game to shoppers. You just need to identify who is in a position to say great things about your product and get them excited about it.

Such gaming greats as Wizards of the Coast founder Peter Adkison and *D&D* inventor Gary Gygax put in hundreds of miles simply driving to every game store in the surrounding states and pitching their games to store owners, employees, and anyone who would listen. After International Games rejected her *Skip-Bo*, Hazel Bowman and her husband drove their motor home to every KOA campground they could find, sharing the game with fellow retirees. After about four years of this, the game had a big enough following that International Games asked her if it was still available. Today *Skip-Bo* remains a bestseller in the mass market.

If you want to get serious about putting your game in front of distributors, retailers, and consumers, you need to go to some conventions. They come in many shapes and sizes throughout the year. The convention year starts with New York Toy Fair, an industry-only event held each February in Manhattan, New York City. It's the biggest game industry show in the world and you pretty much need to be there if you're going to get mass market distribution. It's not recommended for first time self-publishers for several reasons. First, imagine how expensive it must be, then triple that figure. Second, even if you manage to get a good location at the show, it's still difficult to get the attention of the big-name buyers you really want. If you want your game to make an appearance there, it's best to go through a broker.

In March, the GAMA (Game Manufacturer's Association) trade show is an industry-only event that's a good starting place for newcomers to meet distributors and retailers. Plus, it's in Las Vegas, Nevada, so airfare and hotels are cheap. Origins is another big show worth checking out each July in Columbus, Ohio.

If you want to start generating word of mouth among consumers, Gen Con is the best show you can attend. Held each July or August in Indianapolis, Indiana, it's the world's biggest hobby gaming event and it's open to the general public. In fact, many Gen Con attendees are leaders of their local gaming communities throughout North America. Established companies like to debut new products at Gen Con

106

Gen Con Game Convention

because they know if these fans like it, they'll evangelize the new product when they get back home, generating tremendous word of mouth sales in their local communities. Many companies simply give away free products at the show for that very reason. Keep in mind that although there are lots of specialty games there, it's mostly aimed at hobby game products.

The best show in Europe is Essen Spiel, held each October in Essen, Germany. It's a mandatory visit if you want to get noticed by any European publishers and a fascinating contrast to American game conventions. Whereas American conventions are dominated by young males, Europe, and Germany especially, has a much more diverse demographic of game fans. Grandparents, families, even teenage girls come by the hundreds to buy and play strategy games all day—something unheard of in the U.S. Germany has a deeply established tradition of playing board games as family entertainment, and it shows.

When you go to a convention as an exhibitor you'll be expected to rent some space and set up a booth. You can build the booth and ship it there yourself or just rent one from the convention hall like most small companies do. The rest is pretty simple. People walk by and you demo your game to them. Have fun, get excited, get people curious to come over and see what's going on. At a show open to the public you can often pay for all your convention expenses from the games you sell there. If you do, congratulations, you just got a tremendous promotional boost for free. A more detailed listing of the best conventions is available on page 156.

Advertising

Advertising is a sketchy proposition for a self-publisher. There are a few game-oriented magazines you can hit if you think the price is right. If your game is aimed at a certain consumer segment, such as rock climbing fans, you might choose one of their periodicals. If you attend a convention, you also might want to take an ad in the convention guide to draw people to your booth. One option you should consider is sending review copies to editors of gaming periodicals, Web sites, and other places that might write a review of the game. Any press you get is free advertising.

Successful advertising can do several things. It can make people start asking retailers if they carry your game, which is always good. It can drive people to your Web site (if you have one) to learn more about your game. It can also result in direct sales if you don't mind shipping games to consumers one at a time. If you can get your game placed at an online retailer such as Amazon.com or funagain.com your ads may also result in immediate sales. Keep in mind that the sales you generate may not be worth the price of the ads. It's often a matter of both research and trial and error and in the end it often just doesn't make much sense for small self-publishers to advertise in the traditional sense.

Speaking of Web sites, you'll have to decide whether or not you want one. Many self-publishers find the efficiency of communicating information about their product is worth the cost and effort of putting up a Web site. You can find a commercial Web site hosting service for something like $50 a month or cheaper, and you can pay a Web designer anywhere from $400 on up to put one together for you. It's also not that hard to create a Web site yourself if you take some time to learn.

Jeff Grubb, a game designer for 20 years, recalls that even industry leaders have trouble with advertising. "TSR actually spent the money to produce TV ads for *D&D*, then never had the money to buy airtime. They never ran."

Selling

Now that you have the game printed and started getting some promotions under way, it's time to sell some games. Whether your game is Trivial Pursuit or Super Deck (often called the world's worst trading card game) you will probably have to start small. Even the biggest hits of the century start out doing promotions and selling a few copies to consumers here and there until retailers start asking for them. As soon as they're interested and the games start selling well, retailers will start bugging distributors for them. Once distributors take notice your volume will shoot way up. Keep in mind this process can take two, three, four years, or even longer. This is called "pulling" the product through the channel (consumer demand is the driving force) as opposed to "pushing" product through the channel, which happens when publishers try to convince people further down the chain to take the product even though there is no consumer demand yet.

Your biggest potential customers are distributors. If a distributor is really excited about your product, he'll take hundreds or even thousands of them at a time. It's also helpful to approach retailers directly, demo the game to them, and see if you can sell some. Beyond that, there are numerous other, smaller-scale options you can consider, including e-tailing (selling via a Web site), mail-order, booth sales at conventions, catalogs, phone orders from ads in publications, and even eBay or other Web sites.

Distributors

In his seminar for first-time business people, self-publishing veteran Lou Zocchi asks "Have you thought about where you could store 1,000 assembled boxes? *Battle of Britain* boxes measure about 13x10x1.5 inches. 1,000 of them were stacked from floor to ceiling in my living room, and it filled it completely. After we sold 250 games, we managed to craft a tunnel through the boxes to the TV set." He also warns that it's not safe to store them in the garage since there's a high danger of mildew.

Inside a game warehouse

In any case, it's up to you to move the games out of your living room or warehouse door. The first place you should try is distributors. Though they'll buy for a much lower price than a retailer, they'll buy tremendous numbers of copies if they think most retailers will want a few. Sometimes you can sell them some copies based on the strength of the game alone. More often, you'll need to get some retailers excited enough about the game to call them up asking for it. A list of distributors can be found on page 154, but it's also a good idea to go to some conventions and meet some of them in person.

Direct To Retail

It's labor-intensive and time-consuming, but almost every successful self-publisher has had to go through it at some point. You'll have to walk into a game store and sell the manager some games. It's not easy. Be polite, be understanding of their needs, and most of all, be enthusiastic. Sometimes you can offer to demo the game to customers or run a tournament with games sold on a consignment basis. That means you split half of what's sold at the event with the retailer. You need to do whatever you can to demonstrate that the game is going to move off the shelf instead of collecting dust. Sometimes it can be as simple as getting the manager or employees excited about the game. If they're playing and talking about it, chances are they'll convince other people to buy it without even trying. Many of the greatest games started this way, including *Uno*. Players get excited and ask the retailers to carry it, retailers ask distributors, and distributors ask you.

Whether you're pitching to a distributor, retailer, reviewer, or a potential customer, you'll want to have a smooth and fun product demonstration that shows what the game is all about. Demonstrating (called "demoing") gets easier with practice. You'll probably want to plan a little script when you're first starting out. Don't worry about explaining too many of the rules. Get them playing and having a good time as soon as possible, then explain as you go along. Lots of buyers say they don't care whether they win or lose a demo game. Your job is to make them care. I always let them win anyway just in case.

Marketing Organizations and Fulfillment Houses

A new method of getting self-published games to market has become more popular in the last few years. Osseum, Tundra, and Wizard's Attic are all examples of a new breed of organizations designed to pool the resources of many small publishers and help them get their games placed with the bigger retailers and distributors.

Here's how it works. A small game publisher or inventor takes his product to a company like Wizard's Attic. The inventor has the game printed and shipped to the Wizard's Attic warehouse. From there, Wizard's Attic takes care of warehousing, processing customer orders, shipping orders, billing, collecting accounts receivable, processing returns, providing monthly sales reports, and most importantly, listing your game in their trade catalogs, online, and providing them to buyers at sales meetings.

This is an efficient way for a small publisher to get the product to big distributors and into far more stores than would otherwise be possible. The fees charged are generally reasonable. It absolutely makes sense to look one of them up if you're initially planning to run only a few thousand copies. With the increasing popularity of this business model, it's actually becoming somewhat possible to have a day job and run a small publishing business in your spare time.

Wizard's Attic
900 Murmansk St., Suite 7
Oakland CA 94607
wizard@wizards-attic.com
www.wizards-attic.com
800-213-1489

Osseum Entertainment
PO Box 1326
Maple Valley, WA 98038
425-271-5308
jim_fallone@osseum.com
www.osseum.com

Tundra Sales Organization
415 1/2 Division St. S Ste 1
Northfield, MN 55057
woody@tundra-sales-org.com
507-645-2708

For more information on self-publishing I recommend getting the Game Manufacturer's Association's (GAMA's) Manufacturer's Handbook. It gives detailed instructions on business policies, discount structures, freight, bar codes, packaging, solicitation, and numerous other important topics. More information on how to obtain this Handbook is available at www.gama.org, or contact them directly:

The Game Manufacturer's Association
PO Box 1210
Scottsdale, AZ 85252
480-675-0205
gamadesk@gama.org

INSIDER'S VIEW— PUBLISHER AND INVENTOR: WIZKIDS CEO JORDAN WEISMAN

I met with Jordan Weisman, founder and CEO of the wildly successful WizKids. Jordan's company started off with an audacious goal—to create a new hobby miniatures segment in defiance of Games Workshop, whose position in the miniatures market was generally regarded as unassailable. Though they don't release financial information, it's estimated that WizKids will perform in the neighborhood of $20 million a year by its third year of operation.

Brian: "How did you get the idea for *Mage Knight*?"

Jordan: "Well, I've been in the business for 22 years. WizKids is really my fourth company. I have 2 boys who were aged 10 and 8 and I saw they were attracted to miniatures games. The problem was they couldn't play any of them. Even though they wanted to play, they really didn't have the skills to glue the figures together, paint them, and understand all the complex rules. Plus the

Jordan Weisman

112

games were so incredibly slow. There was too much record keeping, too many charts, it was amazing how many problems there were for kids who wanted to get into miniatures games. This stuff just drained out all the visual excitement that the cool-looking minis generated.

"So I started out with the goal of making a game that kids could actually play. I made a list of all those barriers to entry and after noodling on it for a while, I came up with a design that reduced those problems. I looked at trading card games, how accessible they were, how they had quick games with lots of back-and-forth player interaction. If you look at traditional miniatures games they're like—you have lunch while I take my turn, and then I'll go have dinner while you take your turn. Hardly any player interaction during turns. So *Mage Knight* became a game where each player only moves a few figures at once. Lots of back-and-forth.

"I also really like games with evolving, changing conditions during play. That's where the combat dial came from. It's a way to change skills and abilities as the game goes on.

"Then there was the problem of actually getting it all together. I wasn't totally sure it would come out the way it did. I went to China eleven times in the first eight months to get the game manufactured. There were so many issues, getting the quality right, the randomization in the boxes correct, etc."

Brian: "So what makes a game successful?"

Jordan: "The most successful games introduce a new paradigm. The best ones create a new interaction model between the people at the table and the product."

Brian: "What do you mean by that?"

Jordan: "Well, all games are about socialization. That's the primary value of a game. So how do I interact with the product, and how does that change my interaction with the others at the table? Look at Avalon Hill games versus *D&D*. Avalon Hill was traditional war games played on a board. When *D&D* came along it said 'there are no winners or losers. We're going to craft a story.' A totally different way to socialize. Or look at *Magic*; an extremely portable game with simple components—just cards—but incredible depth of strategy. It was a really different way for people to interact.

"Another important thing in the adventure games industry is the fiction, the universe and characters of the game. *BattleTech* actually represented a small paradigm shift since it was the first hybrid roleplaying game and board game. But what really attracted people were the characters and universe. Same with *Shadowrun*, another one of my games. Building a strong intellectual property for your game is important.

"I could also talk a lot about product quality. Pricing is also important. But what I really want to emphasize is community development. As I said, since gaming is about socialization, it's critical to build a positive environment for people to play your game. If you do this right, you create a cadre of evangelists who go out and spread the word of your game at the ground level every single day."

113

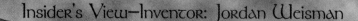

Brian: "So what are some important things game inventors need to know?"

Jordan: "Ask yourself if this is something that entertains you, or something that would entertain a lot of people. Having rules your friends like is great, but exposing it to people who aren't emotionally invested in it is totally different. Try bringing it into game stores and see if you can get people interested in playing who aren't part of your gaming group. You can also run the game at conventions and see how many people want to play.

"Realize that you have the option of bringing your game to a publisher or starting your own game company. The adventure games business is still one of the only industries where you can actually start a company from scratch and have success. There are 5,000 stores in America that are in the games business only because they love it. If it's a good game and gets their attention, they'll pick it up. Unlike those at Target and Wal-Mart, the people at these game stores know about games. Anyone who works at the store will be able to tell you what games are new and cool. They are actually a sales force for you. The creative stuff rises to the top and gets their attention. That's something that just can't happen in the mass market or software industries for example."

Top: Marvel HeroClix: The Hulk, Bottom Left: Marvel HeroClix: The Invisible Woman, Bottom Right: DC HeroClix: Brainiac

114

SECTION FIVE

SELLING A GAME STEP BY STEP

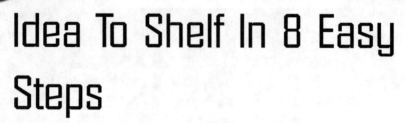

Idea To Shelf In 8 Easy Steps

A quick overview of how the whole thing works:

1. Invent your game. Start with a certain type of consumer in mind.
2. Refine your game. Get people who don't know you to play it. They'll discover more problems than you ever expected. Solve them.
3. Research publishers. Find out what they carry and what they're missing. Target publishers that cater to your chosen consumers.
4. Contact your targeted publishers one at a time. Ask if they're interested in seeing your game. If not, find out why and what they'd rather see instead.
5. If they are interested in your game, send them a prototype or meet with the buyer to give a demonstration.
6. Wait to hear the company's decision.
7. Get feedback and continue development until you make a sale.
8. Negotiate a contract and let the publisher take it to market.

Chapter 20

How To Invent A Game

Target Market

Usually the first thing publishers want to know is "Who is this game for?" Kids? Teens? College students? Families? Boys or girls only? Is it something consumers are going to want to buy for themselves or will it more likely be a gift item? The answer to this question will almost single handedly decide which publishers are most likely to be interested. Generally, publishers have an expertise with a certain type of consumer and relationships with distributors in that market.

Keep in mind that you have to sell your game to a publisher who has to sell it to a distributor who has to sell it to a retailer who has to sell it to a consumer. There are lots of cases where this chain breaks down and publishers and distributors reject an idea that goes on to become a huge hit. Likewise, one need only look at some of the insipid trash that makes it to the game store shelves to see products that publishers thought were good but consumers avoided like week-old tuna casserole.

It helps all parties in this chain to put themselves in the consumer's shoes if they can immediately identify who that consumer is.

Game designer Ryan Miller says, "How do you design a good game? Design with a market in mind. You have to be part inventor and part marketing analyst. You've got to be a little mercenary."

Competing Products

I've heard some designers say they never look at games that are similar to the one they're working on because they don't want outside ideas to influence their original thinking. This is a big mistake. You absolutely need to know what other games are aimed at the same consumer segment you're targeting. First, you don't want to waste your time creating a game that's already been published.

Peggy Brown, Vice President of Marketing for Patch Products commented, "One of the most frequent mistakes we see from new inventors is they just don't know the market. A lot of times they reinvent things already out there. They don't do their research." This not only wastes your time, it tarnishes your future credibility if you ever want to show another game to that publisher.

Second, to understand consumer's needs you need to see what has been successful and what has not. Put the trading card games *Legend of the Five Rings* and *Legend of the Burning Sands* next to each other and they appear very similar, but the first was a hit and the second was a major flop. You need to know why so you don't repeat the mistakes of others.

Further, there are some categories dominated by games no publisher in his right mind wants to compete with. *Scrabble* has such a strong hold on the market that almost no one will publish board

117

games in which players build words. Similarly, it's pretty certain you won't be able to find a publisher for a fantasy-themed trading card game as long as *Magic* dominates that field. In general, if one product has over 50% market share in an industry, it will be tough to challenge. In a case like this the new game would probably never make enough money to cover the marketing expenses to convert people from the old game to the new.

Goals For Your Game

What do you want to accomplish by getting your game published? Be honest, now. You need to answer this question before you begin. Is your primary interest to build a name for yourself? To share your creativity? To have fun? To get rich? How will you know when you've succeeded? When you've sold 5,000 copies? When your game makes it to Toys R Us?

The Hook

A hook is a concept that grabs people and makes them want to pick up the box. It's that little something special that makes your game intriguing and different. Go to a game store and look at some of the newer games on the market. See any games that say things like "The game that lets you …" or "The game of …"? That's a hook.

A hook is more than a phrase or tagline on the box. It's a theme, an attitude, or a subject matter that somehow makes the game unique and memorable. A good example is *Zobmondo*, "The crazy 'Would you rather…' game™." The game asks players to answer questions like "Would you rather eat a live tarantula or hold a live wasp in your mouth for one minute?" Without even knowing what the game play is

Pig from the game Pass the Pigs

like, you know from that description that the game going to stimulate all kinds of weird conversation.

Another game with a good hook is perennial favorite, *Pass the Pigs*. At its heart it's a dice game, but instead of rolling dice players roll bouncy little rubber pigs. Scores are based on whether the pigs land on their front or back feet, their ears, or their noses. It's remarkable how a change in theme can turn a fairly humdrum mechanic into a top-selling product.

Chapter 21

Game Design

Reasons People Play Games

What do people want out of a game? When you start designing, think about why someone will want to play it. People play games for lots of different reasons. Let's start with some of the most important ones.

Emotional Payoffs

A key element of any successful game is that moment of glory when a player makes some brilliant move or comes up with just the right answer. In a January 2002, *Inc. Magazine* interview, Whit Alexander and Richard Tait say they designed *Cranium* around a moment when players would "appear smart and funny in front of their friends." "We wanted every team member to high-five their teammate at least once per game," says Tait. "I know that's not a very scientific metric, but that's what we're going for." Every successful game gives players a chance to feel clever, creative, or cool, even if it's the celebration of a six-year-old avoiding the Molasses Swamp in *Candyland*. Those emotional payoffs are what keep people coming back for more.

If you can pick one or more of these payoffs and nail it for a certain type of player, you'll have a hit on your hands.

Socialization

For many, the most important purpose of a game is an excuse to get together with friends and socialize. Even veteran game designers of such deep and time-consuming games as *Dungeons & Dragons* readily admit that half the fun of the game is wisecracking and joking around with your friends.

Laughter

Watch what people do when they play charades. It's not hard to see what the emotional payoff is. The amount of laughter your game generates is a good acid test of whether your game is more strategic or social. Good strategy games make players spend their time thinking silently. Good social games generate noise and laughter.

Strategic Thinking

Strategy games give players a chance to outthink each other. For them the emotional payoff is in feeling brilliant when they see a move their opponent missed or when a well-laid plan finally comes together. The world's best-known strategy games are *Chess* and *Go*. Speak to a master of either of these games and he'll describe his

119

favorite moments with words like elegance and beauty. To the dedicated player these games are like another language and the most famous games are poetry only an expert can understand.

To Express Creativity

Some people like to act silly in front of their friends. Others like to build an unusual *Pokémon* deck, play an obscure word in *Scrabble*, or try a new chess variation they came up with. Playing games can be a form of self-expression similar to creating art or music. Actually, playing games is an easier and more accessible way for people to be creative since it doesn't require much time, equipment, or effort compared to the more widely recognized art forms. If you think about it, how many opportunities do people get to express their personalities in a non-threatening social setting this way?

As A Hobby

Nearly every great game in the industry has a following of fans that play it once a week or more. The most successful are those games designed with a metagame aimed directly at hobbyists. As discussed earlier, "metagame" is an industry term coined by Richard Garfield that describes all the elements of a game a fan can participate in when he's not actually playing the game. This includes collecting, assembling models, trading, discussing strategy, making political deals, and practicing.

Collecting

Some games, like *Pokémon*, are designed for collectors. For them, part of the game itself is trading and hunting down all available cards to complete your collection. The proliferation of licensed versions of *Monopoly* is another good example of games designed for collectors. I'd be willing to bet the proportion of "Elvis Presley" *Monopoly* sets that actually get played is pretty low. Instead, the Elvis fan treats it as a piece of memorabilia for his collection. Some people even collect games that aren't designed to be collected. One European collector I know buys about 50 new games a year at the Essen Spiel convention to add to his current collection of about 2,000 games.

Common Interest

Though it's a fun game in its own right, one of the reasons fans play the *Major League Baseball Showdown* trading card game is that they love baseball and want to learn more about the teams. In fact, part of the product manager's strategy for *Major League Baseball Showdown* is to give players an opportunity to develop their "sports literacy." Once you've studied all the team stats and faced the best teams against each other, you have the knowledge you need to be part of any baseball conversation. For these players the emotional payoff is not only in playing the game, but in using the things they learned as well.

Quick, Convenient Entertainment

120   Apart from emotional benefits, many games have functional benefits over other entertainment choices. They're quicker to play

than watching a movie and less effort than organizing an outing. If you want to take advantage of these benefits, think about how much effort your consumer is willing to invest to learn your game. Wizards of the Coast game designer Mark Rosewater says, "Easy is hard. Most people don't realize how difficult it is to create a simple, elegant design that is easy for people to start playing right away."

The Classic Game of Chess

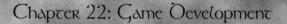

Chapter 22

Game Development

Design Vs. Development

Professionals often differentiate between these two stages of game creation. Design refers to the earlier processes of actually putting the game concept and rules together. Development is the process of working on the details—making sure each strategy is balanced, looking for rules loopholes, and playtesting. Designers answer questions like, "What should you have to do to win?" Developers answer questions like, "Should this figure move six inches per turn or eight?"

Playtesting

I can't emphasize enough how important it is to have your game playtested. Paul Randles, inventor of *Pirate's Cove*, played his first game more than a hundred times over the course of its development. The feedback he got from this process gave him such a deep understanding of players' needs that not only did he sell the game to the first publisher who looked at it, but he was able to develop and sell his next game in far less time. When Richard Garfield began work on *Magic* he had a ready-made playtesting group in his bridge club, a group that later turned out to be essential for developing the game.

A smart, reliable group of playtesters is worth its weight in gold. Putting together a regular playtest group can be a fun way to get together with friends every so often and work on game ideas at the same time. Behind almost every one of the inventors profiled in this book is a playtest group that helped him weed out the mediocre ideas. Paul Randles remarked, "Great games don't come solely from great ideas. They come from several brilliant minds working together on development."

In his book *Game Plan*, Steve Peek advised game designers not to trust anyone's opinion unless you think they would honestly tell you your baby is ugly. While it's great to playtest with friends and family, you also need to make sure you get critical feedback from people you don't know. Have one of your friends take it to her family and make sure they don't know you invented it. Better yet, get someone to play it with people you don't know while you listen from the next room.

Is Development Finished?

How do you know when your game is ready for its first audition? Before you start showing your game to publishers, you should know the answers to the questions on this checklist:

1. Who is it for?
2. Is it easy enough for the target audience to learn?
3. Does it take the right amount of time to play?

122

4. Are the rules clear and concise?
5. Does it have extra parts it doesn't need?
6. How much do you think it should cost?
7. Is your prototype inviting and easy to use if you're not present to explain how to play it?
8. What will make a customer want to pick this game up and buy it?
9. What other games are similar to it?
10. Is it fun?

INSIDER'S VIEW—TOP 10 WORST ACTUAL GAME SUBMISSIONS

...that I've ever seen. (Names have been changed)

10. Regional Trivia of Iowa City (Exactly what it says.)

9. International Politics ("Go Fish" with pictures of foreign presidents on the cards.)

8. Star Empires (A quote from the game description: "Players need only know a small amount of simple calculus to accurately plot their ships' trajectories.")

7. Serving Time (The game of serving a prison sentence.)

6. Scratchers (An Internet game where you can't advance until you go to the store and buy cards that you scratch off to reveal a secret code that you type into your computer.)

5. Terrorists, Inc. (Players move around the board trying to kill people. Think anyone might find it offensive?)

4. The Game Game (A game where players sit down and decide what the rules are going to be, then play the new game they just made up.)

3. Dr. Love (Move around the board to see how many women you can "hook up" with in a single night.)

2. My Mother's Life (Learn the fascinating story of this guy's mother. Thrill as she reveals which laundry detergent she's allergic to.)

1. Monopoly 2 (Just like regular *Monopoly*, but better!)

Chapter 23

Targeting Publishers

The Reality Of Submitting To Publishers

As the concept acquisitions lead at Wizards of the Coast, I review about 150 game ideas a year. Of those 150, we only actually play a dozen or so. Surprised? Don't be. If you've read the interviews of publishers, you've heard them complain about many of the same mistakes that come up repeatedly. If you avoid them you can put your game ahead of 90% of submissions almost immediately.

Another major factor in choosing to look at your game is whether or not you've been published before. If you've already had a successful game released, your new game will probably at least get played. It's a Catch-22 situation that comes up in lots of creative endeavors; they don't want to publish you unless you're a proven success, but you can't prove yourself unless you get published. Just like a first-time author or TV actor, you'll have to overcome this problem through a combination of resourcefulness, talent, and perseverance. Just remember that once you've done it, things get somewhat easier.

You also gain some amount of credibility for having a unique connection to a certain theme. A veteran firefighter sent us a game about battling wildfires. We were intrigued that he might have some interesting insights into the topic. It didn't get far, but we at least played it.

Game designer Jonathan Tweet points out, "When evaluating outside submissions, I look for a sign that the designer was trying to accomplish something. Many people design by intuition and end up with games that seem random or too baroque. The rules should be elegant and clean, and I should know what ends they are trying to accomplish."

Top 10 Reasons Games Get Rejected

1. Poor gameplay. Lots of submissions just aren't fun to play.

2. Unoriginal mechanics. Poor inventors use play elements stolen from a traditional game or a competitor's game, whether intentionally or unintentionally. While no game is 100% original, it shouldn't feel like something we've played before.

3. Submitting a game that's not appropriate for that company. We see games all the time for categories we just don't publish. Either people don't do their research or are hoping a wargame company will change their minds and publish a preschool game.

4. Too focused on theme, not gameplay. Many inventors like the idea of using a certain intellectual property or theme, but don't have the time or talent to put together a compelling game. Instead, they take a traditional game like *War* or *Go Fish*, introduce a board, and slap some

125

pretty pictures of Barbie on it. If a publisher wanted to do a product like that, they wouldn't need an inventor to show them how.

5. Game submitted without required legal forms or with inventor's legal forms. If the company asks you to sign a disclosure form and you don't, your submission goes right in the trash. Asking a publisher to sign a confidentiality agreement usually has the same effect. This is like stamping "I don't understand the procedure" on the front of your submission.

6. Poor marketing potential. Some games are aimed at a consumer segment that's too narrow. Jonathan Tweet recalls a woman who wanted to do a game based on her experiences hanging out at the burger joint in the 1950s when she was in high school. How many people are going to be interested in that today?

7. Not feasible to produce. New inventors tend to overdesign games with too many rules and too many extraneous components. If your game has lots of pieces or anything that would be complicated to manufacture, ask yourself if it's absolutely necessary.

8. Game depends on an unobtainable license. Sure it would be nice to do a *Star Wars*-themed board game, but Hasbro has the license locked up for the foreseeable future. Even if it were available, very few publishers could afford the licensing fees. If your game depends on a license, you need to make sure the license is available and affordable before you pitch.

9. Unclear rules. It's a little-known truth that rules are unbelievably tricky to write. If you want to see what I mean, watch someone try to play your game

A prototype copy of a new game

126

for the first time from your rules while you say absolutely nothing. If a publisher has that much trouble, he's just going to quit.

10. Competes directly with another product in the company. It's like trying to sell an idea for a soft drink that's just like Coke to the Coca-Cola Company.

Deciding On A Publisher

Deciding which publishers you're going to target should be straightforward as long as you know your needs. You want a publisher that meets the following criteria:

1. They publish games that are different from yours, but are aimed at the same target market. These publishers already have good distribution in places where those consumers shop and will be most receptive to a game like yours.

2. They have the financial and technical capability to produce your game. If you've got electronic components like buzzers and flashing lights, many smaller publishers won't have experience doing this kind of product. Lots of companies, especially roleplaying game companies, tend to be very specialized at doing only one kind of game.

3. They publish numerous new titles each year. Some companies, such as Games Workshop, use internal designers almost exclusively. The majority of their business comes from expansions for existing games. These companies aren't likely to look at new submissions at all.

4. They don't publish any games that would directly compete with yours. If they print a game whose main selling points match yours entirely, they are your competitor, not your publisher.

Of course one of the biggest factors publishers consider when looking at your game is whether they've worked with you in the past. Certainly if you've designed a game for them before and it did all right, your chances increase a hundredfold. Even if you're still unpublished, have sent them decent submissions before, acted professionally, and listened to their feedback, your game will still get played before those of first-time submitters.

There are some exceptions to the above guidelines. If you personally know someone at a company or if you want to try to place your game in a non-traditional market, you should feel free to try unorthodox strategies. One inventor got her baby shower game placed in a nationwide maternity clothing store chain. If you have a similar product strategy, don't worry about where a publisher's current distribution is. You'll likely want to start with the smaller specialty publishers.

127

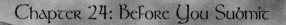

Chapter 24

Before You Submit

Where Do I Start?

By this point you should have decided what kind of consumer your game is targeting. Next, you should have designed and developed your game, including plenty of playtesting. You should also have done some research on the companies that publish games aimed at a similar consumer and should have a few companies in mind. You should also have a playable prototype ready to send out if requested. If you're going to contact an agent, you should do so now. If not, it's time to start contacting publishers directly.

An Agent

An agent or broker is required if you're submitting to top mass market publishers such as Mattel or Hasbro. The biggest publishers are the only ones that look at materials exclusively from industry professionals, returning submissions from the general public unopened.

If submitting to a hobby game publisher or a European company, an agent can be helpful, though it's not necessary. If you don't get an agent for a hobby game or European submission it means you'll be doing more research on companies, creating sales materials to impress buyers, and possibly traveling to conventions to pitch ideas. This can be an important consideration if you're creating a game for the European market and you don't speak German or don't have the money to make several trips.

You shouldn't get an agent for the specialty game market. This market is small enough that most publishers are happy to deal directly with inventors. Further, sales are small enough that most reputable brokers know they can't make much money off the percentage of sales they could expect, so they generally stay away. Disreputable brokers, however, are happy to take specialty games since they make most of their money off submission fees, not percentages of sales. Any agent that's even willing to take on a specialty game is best avoided.

If you decide to look into obtaining an agent, make sure to contact several of them. Most either have Web sites or are happy to answer questions over the phone. Here are some questions you should ask when choosing an agent.

1. What submissions have you placed in the past, and with whom?
2. Do you represent any submissions or only ones that meet certain standards? What are the standards?
3. How many companies will you be able to show the game to?

128

4. When will you be able to show it?

5. What are your submission fees, if any?

6. If you place the game with a publisher, do you take a percentage, and if so, how much?

   Look out for agents that represent any product, regardless of quality, and that charge submission fees of $500 or more. On the other hand, don't be alarmed if an agent charges 30% to 60% of your royalties as a fee. You want someone who makes their money from percentages of sales—they are far more likely to sell it to a large publisher. You'd much rather get 50% of $100,000 than 90% of $10,000.

   Check page 155 in the back of the book for a list of reputable agents. Don't rule out an agent just because he or she is not on the list—there are plenty of other good ones out there. Make some phone calls and choose the one that makes you the most comfortable.

Chapter 25

Eight Submission Strategies

Research

Researching your target company is essential for any game you want to sell. At the very least you need to know what kind of products the company makes. While you're at it, check the company's Web site to see if they have posted their submission policies. Often companies will provide "how to" instructions for sending in proposals. Follow them. By the way, even if they say they don't accept submissions, that doesn't mean you have to give up. You might be able to try another strategy with that company.
Recommended for: All games, all companies.

Cold Call

Sometimes you can just call up a small company and ask them to look at your game idea. It's an easy way to get direct information on what kind of products they're looking for. If the idea sounds interesting they'll give you instructions on how to send it in. Even if they're not interested they'll probably be able to recommend other companies you could contact. If you try this with medium-sized or large companies you'll most likely get a curt brush-off.
Recommended for: Small specialty game companies.

Query Letter and Phone Call

This method demonstrates that you understand professional protocol. Write a letter introducing yourself and your concept and asking if you can speak to them on the phone. Give the person time to respond. If you get a positive response or no response, call them up. You need to know the name of the person you're sending the letter to. One way to do this is call the receptionist and ask who's in charge of marketing or product development. Ask him to spell that person's name. Then address your letter to that person.
Recommended for: Medium-sized and large companies in all markets.

E-mail Inquiry and Phone Call

This method is similar to the query letter and phone call, and in many cases is superior since it's easier for them to respond to e-mail than a letter. You still need to craft your query e-mail as well as you would a letter. Unfortunately, it can be more difficult to get the e-mail address of the right person to send it to. Again, you can talk to the receptionist or someone in customer service to get the right

130

e-mail address.

Recommended for: Mid-sized companies in all markets.

Broker

Getting a broker or agent is the easiest way to sell a game. In exchange for 30% to 60% of your royalties, a broker essentially does the hard work for you and uses his contacts to get your game in front of the best companies. Unfortunately, most good brokers are picky about what games they will take. Check out the list of brokers on page 155 and contact them for submission guidelines.

Recommended for: Mass market games, and on occasion, the larger European and hobby game companies.

Approach In Person

This means conventions and trade shows. Don't show up unannounced at anyone's office. Ask who looks at new ideas, find that person, and introduce yourself. Ask if you can talk about a new concept. They may or may not want to look at it there, but just establishing that you're polite and professional goes a long way towards getting your foot in the door.

Recommended for: European, specialty game, and sometimes hobby game publishers.

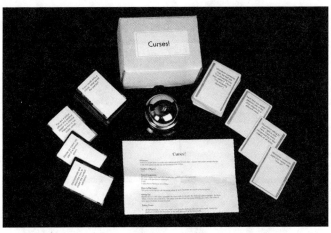

The prototype of Curses!

Networking

Networking is the most difficult, time-consuming, and most effective method of contacting companies without getting a broker. With this strategy, it's all about who you know. Your goal is to get to know the right people. The game industry isn't all that big and lots of people are friends with each other. If you can start hanging out with people

131

in the industry, ask who they know. Arrange introductions. You can build relationships with publishers the same way brokers do. Sometimes you can volunteer to do free work for companies and get to know people that way. **Recommended for:** Hobby and specialty games.

Gimmicks

Sometimes game designers go overboard attempting to catch the reviewer's attention. They'll put a small game in a huge box, wear a funny costume to pitch it, or try to have it delivered with a singing telegram. Gimmicks are risky. A publisher's gut reaction is that if you have a great product you shouldn't need to dress it up. Once in a while a gimmick will work well, but not very often.
Not recommended.

The final product of Curses!

INSIDER'S VIEW— INVENTOR: PAUL RANDLES

Paul was a manager for a game company who decided he was done with publishing other peoples' games and with no previously published titles of his own, became a respected game designer in the European market within two years. In 2000 he sold his first game, *Pirate's Cove*, to the first company he showed it to. He currently has two more games pending release with large publishers.

Paul Randles

Paul is a fervent game fan affectionately nicknamed "Papa Christmas" for his jovial nature and habit of giving out candy at work in order to "make every day a little bit like Christmas." Paul used his time as a product manager to study the life cycles of games firsthand and to meet others in the industry, traveling to conventions as much as possible. Finally, he decided to quit his job and make a serious effort at getting a game of his own published. He and co-designer Dan Stahl started spending evenings brainstorming and testing ideas. On the third try they finally got one they felt was strong enough to pitch.

133

Pirate's Cove is a game of swashbuckling drama and second-guessing opponents. Players sail their ships around the map gathering resources, upgrading equipment, fighting, and digging up treasure. The initial design started in July 2000 and wasn't finished until September. By October they had a prototype and were ready to pitch to publishers. They traveled to Europe to meet publishers in person at the Essen Spiel convention. Amigo, a German publisher that happened to be their first choice, was impressed with the game, and by December agreed to publish it. The game hit the shelves in February of 2001 with the German name *Piratenbucht* and Paul received his first royalty check in July 2001.

Piratenbucht

The secret of Paul's success? "I start out by picking a company first. I figure out what kind of game that company is going to want to see and start from there." How does he find out what they want? "Sometimes you can look at their product line and see what they're missing. A much better way, what I always try to do, is talk to the buyer and ask them. I was able to attend enough events that I met the best buyers in person. It makes a huge difference."

Paul relates his strategy, "I decided early on that I only wanted to show publishers the best of the best stuff I come up with. That means I have to generate a ton of ideas and then reject most of it myself—which is not easy. I get lots of games to the playtesting stage and then throw them out. The benefit is that publishers now look forward to a high level of quality from me. When I'm showing them my new games they're actually excited to see them.

"There are a couple of ways you can approach design. One is the 'mechanic approach,' where the game is about some abstract interaction of pieces or resources. This is easy to design but hard to sell. Another way to do it is the 'theme approach,' where the game is an interesting simulation of a real-world event like the growth of cities in *Carcassonne*. This kind of game is very hard to design but easy to sell if you do it right."

134

Chapter 26

Contacting Publishers

Contacting Mass Market Publishers

After her idea was rejected, one woman sat in the lobby of a mass market publisher's corporate office every day from morning until closing time, waiting for the buyer to walk out to his car so she could plead with him to change his mind. Eventually it got bad enough that the buyer had to call the police to cart her off. Even then she came back a few times. No wonder the mass market publishers are the toughest to break into. Because they have the highest visibility of any game company catagory in the world, they are the target of every crackpot who thinks he has the next *Monopoly*. This category does command the kind of sales figures that could make an inventor rich. For these reasons, mass market publishers put up formidable barriers to the general public. With Hasbro and Mattel, you likely won't be able to get your game in front of a buyer unless you go through an agent they trust. Most people don't mind paying an agent a percentage of royalties since getting published in the mass market will typically help a game sell twenty to thirty times the number of games published elsewhere.

Because there are relatively fewer publishers in the mass market there are also fewer options once the top companies have declined your game.

Contacting Hobby Game Publishers

Hobby game companies vary quite a bit in how difficult they are to approach. Generally speaking, the bigger the company, the more difficult it will be to get your idea in the door. Nevertheless, a polite and professional approach will certainly give you a decent shot at speaking with a buyer in most hobby game companies. Tony Lee, former Creative Director for Third Rail Games, commented, "The best thing you can do is get to know people. Talk to them, let them know you understand their needs and aren't some freaky nut." A good approach is attending hobby game conventions like Origins and Gen Con. You might get the opportunity to meet buyers and vice-presidents alike from almost all the companies in the industry. While they likely won't be interested in taking a look at your game then and there, you can still ask questions about the submissions process, get a phone number, and ask if they would take a look if you send it to them in a few weeks. Most people in the hobby game industry are passionate, even fanatical about games. Keep this in mind when you talk to them. You'd better know something about the major games in the industry, and especially the games that company publishes, if you want to be taken seriously.

Many hobby game companies were formed by people who wanted to publish their own games. That doesn't mean they won't publish yours, it just means they are going to give first priority to their own ideas. If you are willing to do some free development work on some of their ideas first you might be able to create some

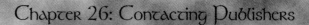

opportunities for your own ideas later on in the process.

Role-playing games (abbreviated RPGs) are an exception to most of these rules. There's a steady market for role-playing game supplements, rulebooks, classes, monsters, adventures, and sourcebooks, especially for established lines like *D&D*. Publishers big and small are often looking for new talent. The surest way to get involved in this industry is to start small and work up. Look for some small publishers, contact them directly, and ask if they'll look at your work. There are enough small publishers out there that your chances of success are quite high if you have some talent, you check your grammar, and you persevere. Another recommended option is to read the submissions guidelines for industry periodicals like *Dragon* and *Dungeon* magazines. If you can get some articles published, your chances of getting other original material goes up tremendously. In fact, some people who started out this way now make a living from freelance role-playing game assignments or have even been hired full time to write RPG materials.

Contacting American Specialty Game Publishers

The good news is that this category is the easiest to get started. The better news is that dozens of new games in this category are published every year and publishers are hungry for fresh new ideas.

Contacting them is straightforward. Once you've selected a publisher, send a cover letter (see page 160 for an example of a cover letter) or call them up and ask about their submission policy. If you've done your homework you'll have given the publisher all the information they need to make a judgment on whether it's a good fit for them. Very often they'll evaluate the concept right away and let you know whether or not they're interested in playtesting it.

Contacting European Game Publishers

Paul Randles, inventor of *Pirate's Cove* puts it best, "You have to know someone, but it's not that hard to get to know someone." You can very often approach buyers at industry shows like Essen Spiel and the Nuremburg Toy Fair. Again, it's not likely they'll want to look at your game right there, but you can still get some submission advice and a promise to open your package in a few weeks, which is all you really need. When a publisher can look you in the eye and judge whether or not you're going to be easy to work with it goes a long way toward establishing your credibility.

Make sure you are able to speak knowledgably about the company's games and the top games in the industry before talking to any buyer. Similar in many ways to buyers in the hobby game market, many European buyers are often game fans first, and businesspeople second. Most European buyers are extremely smart, well-educated, and speak English. A polite, professional letter or phone call can sometimes get you directly to the buyer. Then again, sometimes you'll just get a brick wall.

Most of the time it makes sense to get an agent if you don't plan on making a personal tour of Europe. However, it is possible, though difficult, to place a game with a European publisher through phone and e-mail contact alone.

Networking

Networking is briefly mentioned in the "Eight Submission Strategies" chapter, but it really deserves more attention. If you read the stories of successful inventors, you'll notice that many of them got involved with the games business even before they got published.

Ryan Miller, lead designer of the *Warhammer 40K Collectible Card Game* for Sabertooth Games, relates the story of how he came to be a game designer. "When I was in the army in 1996, I was assigned as a guard at the military prison in Leavenworth, Kansas. I sat for eight hours a day up in a tower watching the yard with nothing but a chair and a rifle. You can't imagine how boring that is. I learned from the prisoners how to make dice out of hardened toilet paper and played *Yahtzee* with myself for hours. I also dreamed up a lot of game ideas. After I was done I wanted to work on games so badly I moved to Seattle and got a job judging tournaments for $6 an hour at the Wizards of the Coast Game Center. I met contacts there that led to a job at the corporate headquarters. There I met Bob Watts, who founded Sabertooth and who liked my prison-era game idea enough to hire me and publish it. My advice is never throw your old notebooks away and never give up."

Jeff Grubb has been a game designer for 20 years, with published card games, board games, computer games, role-playing games, and 14 novels under his belt. His advice, "Sometimes games happen by serendipity, but you have to know people in the industry. In the hobby industry that means going to cons [conventions]. Tracy Hickman wrote some material based on *D&D* called Ravenloft. He sold photocopied versions of it at Gen Con. He eventually met Mike Gray, who was then at TSR. Mike looked at the copies and said 'This is a violation of copyright. It's also pretty good.' So they hired him. It takes time, but building contacts and networking is worth it."

Chapter 27

Protecting Your Property

Trademarks, Copyrights, and Patents

If you look deeply into this topic, there is a lot of conflicting advice about whether or not you should obtain trademarks, copyrights, or patents for your game. After a while it becomes clear that most of the people in favor of these legal protections are lawyers, while most of the people who advise against them are publishers and experienced inventors. I'm both a publisher and an experienced inventor, so guess which side I'm on?

Simply put, if you're pitching to established game publishers, trademarks and patents are so difficult to obtain and enforce in the game industry that they're often useless. Copyrights are easier to obtain, and are probably worth getting in many cases, but don't really offer the protection most inventors want. All these legal tools were specifically designed to protect brand names, technological developments, and artistic works, none of which fit games very well.

What's the difference among the three? In brief, trademarks are used to protect unique names and phrases that are linked to your product. Patents protect tools and other devices that perform a function, while copyrights protect your specific written material or artwork.

Trademarks are intended to keep other companies from using your product's name or tagline, such as "The Game of Verbal Explosions™" (*Outburst*) or "The Game of Global Domination™" (*Risk*). As such, they're not too useful until your game is actually getting published unless you think your game's name is so good that someone might steal it and stick it on another game.

Patents, especially those that merely combine existing ideas in new ways, are notoriously slow, expensive, and difficult to get approved. When WizKids released *Mage Knight* in 2000, they filed a patent application to protect their miniatures' clickable bases, which happened to be one of the most innovative devices to hit the game industry in years. As of this book's publication, it's still "patent pending," the application sitting in some clerk's filing cabinet somewhere. Even when approved, many concepts used in gaming don't fit patent requirements well. There are many existing patents that, if challenged, would likely fail to protect the patent holders since definitions of game components are vague when held up to legal scrutiny. Plus, the patent holder is in charge of enforcing it. This means if someone violates your patent you have to take them to court at your own expense. Patents really aren't the right legal tools to protect games.

Copyrights protect only an author's specific literary, artistic, or musical expression. Copyright law makes it clear that ideas, methods, and names are not copyrightable. That means you can copyright any artwork or passages of prose that appear in the game, but you can't copyright the basic idea of the game. On the plus side, it's not too hard to get a copyright.

To register a copyright, you need to put these three things in a

single package:
1. A completed application form, available on the Internet at: www.copyright.gov or by phone at 202-707-3000.
2. The filing fee (which was $30 in 2002).
3. A copy of the work being registered.

Send all this to:

Library of Congress
Copyright Office
101 Independence Avenue, SE
Washington, DC 20559-6000

Your best protection against idea theft is checking out the reputation of those you're dealing with. If uncertain about a particular company, call up an agent or broker and ask if she knows anything about that company's reputation. In general, it's also not a bad idea to put your name and phone number in small footnote-type at the bottom or back of every page of text and artwork you send. Pages can sometimes get mixed up as they pass over many peoples' desks. You want to make sure it's clear who created what.

If self-publishing, it's another story. When you sell to a company, that company's legal protections cover your game. When it's your own company, you need to at least make sure nobody can take your product's name. Jordan Weisman advises getting whatever protection you can. "It makes sense to protect yourself. Copyrights are cheap, but patents are tens of thousands."

Confidentiality Agreements

My advice on this subject is pretty simple. If a publisher asks you to sign an agreement that protects them from liability, read it carefully, but in most cases you'll want to sign it. If you're thinking about asking them to sign a similar one protecting you, don't. This may seem unequal (it is) and unfair (it's not).

Publishers see enough submissions that they don't need to bother with people who won't follow directions, but that's not the only reason you should play by their rules. Game companies don't stay in business by ripping off inventors, and experienced inventors know it. When you question their legal forms it marks you as someone who's a pain in the neck to work with. A company simply can't expose itself to liability by making any agreement that might imply an inventor owns an idea. Corporations make appealing legal targets and publishers are obligated to take steps to protect themselves from lawsuits filed by people who are either misguided or scam artists.

Richard Garfield relates, "Companies didn't get into the business to make money off other people's games. They did it to make their own games."

The worst-case scenario—that a company steals your idea and makes a fortune without paying you for it—is unlikely. But there's a far more dangerous worst-case scenario that happens over and over again—an inventor is overprotective of his idea and it never gets published because he's afraid of it getting stolen.

139

Chapter 28

What To Do If They Don't Say Yes

How Much Waiting Is Too Much?

Game companies aren't known for their speedy correspondence and prompt return of phone calls. It can sometimes be downright aggravating waiting to hear a decision. Most companies ask for six to eight weeks to decide whether or not they're interested. Other companies play all their games for the year during a certain couple of months. Make sure you find out when you'll be hearing back at the same time you make your submission. In any case, the chances of hearing back by the time they say they'll call you are about 50/50. So what should you do once the time is up? The wrong thing to do is call or e-mail every day. A better idea is to pick a time when your contact is likely to be available and call once a week, every week at the same time. The polite but persistent approach is the one that publishers respond to best.

Option Agreements

Option agreements are for those companies that just can't make up their minds. If a company has had your game for more than the customary maximum of eight weeks and you're getting impatient, you can suggest an option agreement. When a company signs one, they pay you a flat fee for the opportunity to keep anyone else from getting it for a specified length of time. Once the time is up, they have either decided to publish it or give it back to you and you can take it elsewhere.

Option agreements are most common among large companies dealing with experienced inventors. If you ask a smaller company to sign they're more likely to say, "Oh that's ok we'll just send it back without looking at it then." In any case, it doesn't hurt to ask. (You can find a sample option agreement on page 166.)

Trying Again

Tried your favorite publisher, but no dice? (So to speak.) Lather, rinse, repeat. It's rare to get published on your first submission, so keep at it with other publishers in the same market. Make sure to ask for feedback when they review your game and address these issues when you submit to the next company.

Especially difficult is the mass market. If your game makes the rounds of the top publishers with no results, you have four options:

140

1. Redesign your game and try again.
2. Wait for a few years until market conditions change and pitch it again.
3. Look at publishing it in another market.
4. Self-publish.

Keep in mind that placing a game in the mass market is very hard—harder than getting into the most exclusive university. There is simply not enough retailer shelf space to place every deserving game that comes along. Sometimes you need a lot of good luck as well as a good game. Thankfully, you can always try again later. People change positions in companies and the next person may be more receptive.

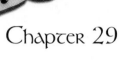

Chapter 29

What To Do If They Do Say Yes!

Negotiating A Contract

What a great position to be in! The fact that they want your game but don't yet have it gives you the negotiating advantage here. In fact, a publisher is more inclined to respect an inventor who has a clear understanding of his game's worth. In any case, before you accept or reject the first number they float by you, there are several ways you can improve the offer without even discussing dollars. You might try exploring the following options with your publisher:

1. Opportunities to design sequels or expansions if the game meets certain sales thresholds.
2. A shorter expiration date for the licensing agreement, so that if the game takes off you can license it to an even bigger publisher.
3. Free copies of the game for you and your playtesters. You will probably want at least 15 or 20, but more never hurts.
4. Travel and accommodations for conventions and trade shows to promote the game.
5. Freelance development work on this game or other games they may have in the pipe.

If your publisher agrees to any of these terms, make sure to get them in your contract.

If you are in the enviable position of having two companies interested in the game at the same time, you have gigantic negotiating power. This is not recommended for first-time inventors, since a botched deal can affect your reputation in the industry, and reputations don't recover quickly.

How Much Money Should I Get?

Almost all game publishers pay inventors in royalties as a percentage of wholesale sales. In general, the bigger the company, the smaller the royalty will be. A small company might go as high as 10% to 12%, while the biggest mass market publishers might pay a first-timer 4% or less.

The second factor in how much they'll be willing to pay is how hot they think your game is and how hot they think you are. After inventing some of the best-selling games in the world, Brian Hersch was able to negotiate royalties of up to 15%, even with the biggest publishers. The fact that he'd formed relationships with rival companies and produced so many best-selling games gave him a strong negotiating position.

Every part of the payment agreement should be spelled out clearly in your licensing contract. Don't make any verbal agreements without getting the details signed in writing first. (A sample licensing contract is available on page 164.)

Keeping A Handle On Your Rights

You never know what's going to happen. People quit, and companies can go out of business or run out of cash unexpectedly. Putting an expiration date on the licensing agreement is important to limit the trouble you'll be in if a company goes belly up or the CEO goes crazy. You also might consider a provision in the contract that stipulates the rights will return to you if the game isn't on the market by a certain date.

143

Chapter 30

The Game Industry's Dirty Little Secret

You're bound to find out sooner or later, so you might as well know now. Talented businesspeople go into investment banking, not games.

That doesn't mean every product manager is an idiot. The most successful companies are still on top partly because they have the best managers. But the history of game companies is littered with stories of incompetent executives who made laughably bad product decisions and strategic mistakes while everyone else cringed helplessly in horror. As a successful inventor, sooner or later you are likely to run into the vice president who insists on adding ponies and rainbows to your World War I trench warfare game so little girls will like it.

Every publisher has a shameful decision they try to forget. Even the biggest toy company in the world, Mattel, made one of the worst business moves in history when it bought the world's second largest consumer software company, The Learning Company, for over $3.5 billion in 1999. Only a year later, The Learning Company was losing $1.5 million a day and Mattel was forced to sell it for about $60 million. That's around $3.44 billion flushed down the toilet in one year.

There are lots of snafus at smaller companies as well, though most of them are kept under wraps by public relations departments. Industry insiders are privy to all kinds of stories that the general public usually never hears.

Mike Selinker, longtime TSR game designer, recalls a number of troubles the company had during its decline from the colossus of the industry to its near-death experience. In 1993, *Magic* became an overnight phenomenon, and TSR felt the need to react in kind. They sent two designers into a secret lab for a week. Within six weeks they had put an entire trading card game together using scraps of artwork from previously published games. There was basically no playtesting. In cases where they needed new art, they took photos of employees dressed up in costumes. The game was *Spellfire*, one of the most ridiculed trading card games in the business, and a product that severely damaged TSR's reputation as an industry leader.

Dragon Dice was another case of weak business analysis. The story goes that TSR's president made a visit to Hong Kong where the product was manufactured. The vendors appealed to the president's sense of pride, pointing out that other companies were placing much bigger manufacturing orders. If TSR were a respectable company, they said, it would manufacture at least a million copies of *Dragon Dice*. Ego at stake, the president agreed, "OK, print it!" A million copies were printed on that whim, and only 200,000 sold for a financial loss of around

144

$8 million.

In 1998, a top role-playing game company that also published books sent a fantasy novel to the printers but left out one small detail … they forgot to include the last six chapters. By the time someone discovered the mistake the entire print run had been manufactured and delivered to their warehouses. Calling it a disaster would be an understatement. Scrapping the ruined books would destroy the distribution schedule and waste tens of thousands of dollars. The product manager's first reaction was to blame the printers, but once the printers conclusively proved it was the game company's fault, there wasn't much he could do. Ever resourceful, the product manager looked at the book and said, "Well, you know, the book still reads okay without the last six chapters…" They shipped it to bookstores without telling anyone. I have no idea how well it sold.

One executive at a smaller game company in the 1980s got involved with illegal substances. At some point he decided to use the company checkbook to write a check for psychedelic mushrooms. This fact would probably never have been discovered if one of the partners in the business hadn't decided to take a look at the company finances before sending them to the accountant. There was listed the check number, dollar amount, and the accounting entry "For Drugs." Probably not tax deductible.

One game company had trouble trying to deal with the explosive growth that comes with a runaway hit. The business was growing so quickly that new people were being hired almost every day. To deal with all these new hires, the company acquired a new payroll software system to automate distribution of paychecks. In order to get employee data entered as quickly as possible, the president's assistant went to each person's desk and personally confirmed every employee's name, position, and salary. Everything seemed to be working smoothly. Nearly a year later, the manager of the art department came to the president to complain about a certain employee named Lawrence. "He isn't even working on any projects, and all he does is order expensive computer equipment and charge it to the company," the art manager complained. The president replied, "Well, he reports to you, doesn't he? Get him in shape or fire him." The art manager shook his head. "Lawrence doesn't report to me, he reports to the Vice President." The VP was immediately called in. "What's up with Lawrence?" asked the president, "It seems like he's not doing any work!" "Lawrence doesn't report to me," the VP replied, puzzled, "he reports to the art manager." The three of them stared at each other in silence. Lawrence had actually just wandered into the office and happened to be standing around when the assistant came by asking for each person's title and salary information. He'd made up a job title, made up a salary, and by finding a desk and looking busy, he'd managed to collect a paycheck for almost a year. He was let go that day.

Conclusion

Let's face it, none of us are doing any interstellar travel in our lifetimes. Until we do, I believe that the last true frontier is the human imagination. The Christopher Columbuses of our century, the people who open up new worlds for us, are the J.R.R. Tolkiens, the George Lucases, and the Gary Gygaxes. Creative people like these take us places we've never been, invent new ways for us to interact, and give us tools to look at the world in different ways. The amazing thing is, anyone with an imagination can do it. With any luck, this book has inspired you to delve deeply into your own imagination, to build your design skills, and to improve your ability to critically evaluate new ideas.

I believe strongly that games are a powerful force for good in the world. If you sell 15,000 copies of a four-player game and each one only gets played once for 20 minutes, you have created 20,000 hours of laughter, joy, and togetherness for people. That's something worth doing.

In the end though, it really doesn't matter if you ever sell a game or not. Creating a game is a form of self-expression, like painting, writing, filmmaking, or music. If you find it compelling, interesting, and beautiful, you should play and enjoy your game whether or not it meets the criteria of the marketplace. Some of the most meaningful poems ever written were never published, but written in personal letters meant only for the eyes of a loved one. Likewise, a game you design is worth doing for its own sake. Even if you never sell it you should still be proud of this fact: You're a game inventor.

In parting, I leave you with some words from Richard Garfield:

"Here's the best advice I have for game inventors. Have fun every step of the way. Then no matter what happens, you can't lose."

146

SECTION SIX

RESOURCES AND EXAMPLES

Publishers and Manufacturers

O nce you've looked at a company's products on the shelves you can look up their contact information on this list. Keep in mind that not all companies on this list are interested in buying games from inventors. Some of them are even self-publishing inventors trying to get their first product off the ground. Others are printers that only manufacture other people's games. However, all of them have released important products in at least one of the four markets. Remember, you should look at the products a company makes and find out about their business before you contact them.

Adept Press
PO Box 14616
Chicago, IL 60614
847-424-1471

Agents of Gaming Inc.
7672 McEwen Rd.
Dayton, OH 45459
937-436-2412

AleaSteinbichlweg
183233 Bernau/Chiemsee
83233 Germany
+49-0 8051-970721

Aldebaran Imports Inc.
NS1 W17067
Shagbark Rd.
Menomonee Falls, WI 53051
262-252-8793

Alderac
Entertainment Group
4045 Guasti Rd St.
Ontario, CA 91761
909-390-5444

Alliance Games
Distributors LLC
1101 Greenwood Rd.
Baltimore, MD 21208
410-602-8000 x3037

American Board Game
87 West Greenwich Ave.
Roosevelt, LI NY 11575
516-223-8596

American Eagle Games
390 Junell
Reynoldsburg, OH 43068

Amigo SpielWaldstrasse
23 D-5 Dietzenbach
63128 Germany
+49-0 6074 3755-0

Apopis Consortium
41 W 879 Bowlgren Cir.
Elbern, IL 60119
608-255-1348

Atlas Games
PO Box 131233
Roseville, MN 55113
651-638-0077

Avalanche Press Ltd.
PO Box 100852
Birmingham, AL 35210
205-957-0017

Avalon Hill Games
PO Box 707
Renton, WA 98057-0707
425-204-8008

Ballantine Del Rey
201 East 50th St.
New York, NY 10022

Bastion Press
PO Box 46753
Seattle, WA 98146
206-763-3368

Beyond Board Games
37 Wolfe Ave.
Beacon Falls, CT 06403
203-720-2463

Black Dragon Press
1045 Darling St.
Flint, MI 48532-5032
810-239-6410

Boardgames.com Inc.
120 Old Camplain Rd.
Hillsborough, NJ 08844
908-429-0202

Cactus Game Design Inc.
751 Tusquittee Rd.
Hayesville, NC 28904
828-389-1536

Cardinal Industries
21-01 51st Avenue
Long Island City, NY 11101
710-784-3000

Carta Mundi Inc.
10444 Wallace Alley St.
Kingsport, TN 37663
512-777-5172

Chaosium Inc.
900 Murmansk St.
Oakland, CA 94607
510-452-4658

Cheapass Games
5212 NE 60th St.
Seattle, WA 98115
206-526-1096

Chessex
Manufacturing Co Inc.
PO Box 80255
Fort Wayne, IN 46898-0255
260-471-9511

Classic Cards & Games
125 The Masters Circle
Costa Mesa, CA 92627
714-435-1256

Clockworks
5765 73rd Pl. 1st Floor
Maspeth, NY 11378
785-832-2798

Cloud Kingdom Games Inc.
275 Waneka Pkwy #4
Lafayette, CO 80026-2746
303-926-8518

Cold Creek
Publishing Company
PO Box 12636
Pleasanton, CA 94588
253-981-7534 (fax only)

Columbia Games Inc.
PO Box 3457
Blaine, WA 98231
360-366-2228

Comic Images
280 Midland Ave.
Saddle Brook, NJ 07662
201-794-9877

Component Game
Systems Inc.
1313 New Windsor Rd.
New Windsor, MD 21776-9127
607-652-2378

Conquest Games
1122 W Burbank Blvd.
Burbank, CA 91506
818-842-9200

Corsair Publishing LLC
PO Box 259836
Madison, WI 53725-9836
608-275-6888

Courier Publishing
Company Inc.
PO Box 1878
Brockton, MA 02403
508-587-0975

Cranium
2025 First Avenue, Suite 600
Seattle, WA 98121
206-652-9708

The Creator Workshop
6th Floor Fung House 19
Connaught Road Central
Hong Kong
852-2439-5979

Dart Flipcards Inc.
8086 Trans Canada Hwy
St Laurent PQ
H4S 1M5 Canada
514-856-6824

Decipher Games Inc.
253 Granby
St. Norfolk, VA 23510
757-623-3600

Dice & Games Ltd.
Meekings Rd. Chilton
Industrial
Sudbury Suffolk
C010 6XD UK
+44 1787 373501

Dwarven Forge
306 E 51st Street
New York, NY 10022
212-355-4326

Eagle Games Inc.
13731 Capista Dr.
Plainfield, IL 60544
815-577-8920

EuroGames/Descartes
USA Inc.
PO Box 953
Phoenixville, PA 19460
610-917-0311

Evil Polish Brothers LLC
6544 N 13th St.
Phoenix, AZ 85014
602-277-9767

Excelsior Games
PO Box 398
Park Ridge, IL 60068
847-384-0656

Fantasy Flight
Games Inc.
1975 W. County Rd. B2
Suite #1
Roseville, MN 55113
651-639-1905

FASA Corporation
1100 W. Cermack No B-305
Chicago, IL 60608
312 243-5660

Fast Forward
Entertainment
PO Box 239
Delavan, WI 52115
262-728-6501

Five Rings
Publishing Group
PO Box 707
Renton, WA 98057-0707
206-401-9088

Fleer / Skybox
International
1120 Route 73
Mount Laurel, NJ 08054
609-231-5923

Flying Buffalo Inc.
PO Box 1467
Scottsdale, AZ
85252-1467
480-945-6917

Flying Tricycle LLC
1523 Meriline Ave.
Dayton, OH 45410
937-253-0869

Games Workshop (UK)
Willow Rd.
Lenton Nottingham
NG7 2WS UK
0115-916-8109

149

Games Workshop Inc.
Glen Burnie HQ
6721 Baymeadow Dr.
Glen Burnie, MD
21060-6401
410-590-1400

Gamescience Inc.
7604 Newton Dr.
RR9 N. Biloxi, MS
39532-2830
228-392-4177

Gamesource Ltd.
14808 Trend Farmers
Branch, TX 75234
214-358-1633

Gaslight Press
PO Box 2411
Redmond, WA 98073-2411
425-376-0172

Geo-Hex
534 SE Oak St.
Portland, OR 97214-1122
503-288-4805

GMT Games
PO Box 1308
Hanford, CA 93232-1308
847-895-0436

Great American
Puzzle Factory
16 S Main St.
South Norwalk, CT 06854
203-838-4240

Green Knight
Publishing
900 Murmansk St. #5
Oakland, CA 94607
510-302-0391

Green Ronin Publishing
PO Box 1723
Renton, WA 98057-1723
206-725-2839

Guardians of Order Inc.
176 Speedvale Ave. #W
Unit 2
Guelph, Ontario
N1H 2C3 Canada
519-821-7174

Hammerdog Games
1315 1/2 Huestis Ave.
Ft. Wayne, IN 46807
219-456-6547

Hans Im Glück Verlag
Birnauerstrasse 15
München
80809 Germany

Harper Collins Publisher
10 East 53rd Street
New York, NY 10022
212-207-7135

Hasbro Games
50 Dunham Rd.
Beverly, MA 01915
978-927-7600

HekaForge Productions
36460 N U.S. Hwy 45
Lake Villa, IL 60046
847-356-7484

Heliograph Inc. 26
Porter St.
Somerville, MA 02143-221
617-776-3338

Hero Games
300 Balthusrol Dr.
Aptos, CA 95003-3406
415-786-6774

Hogshead Publishing Ltd.
18-20 Bromell's Rd.
London
SW4 0BG UK
44-0207-207-5490

Holistic Design Inc.
5295 Highway 78 Ste. D-337
Stone Mountain, GA 30083
770-592-1718

Human Head Studios Inc.
6325 Odana Rd.
Madison, WI 53719
608-298-0643

Image Crafters
2606 S. Durango
North Las Vegas, NV 89117
702-655-8043

Inner City Games Designs
36460 North Hwy 45
Lake Villa, IL 60046
847-356-7484

Interactive Imagination
PO Box 4710
Seattle, WA 98104
206-264-7598

Iron Crown Enterprises
112 Goodman St.
Charlottesville, VA 22902
434-244-0881

JDB Games
11100 Prospect Ave. NE
Albuquerque, NM 87112
505-294-4751

Jolly Roger Games
PO Box 61
Sigel, IL 62462
217-844-4448

Journeyman Press
11 Malcolm Hoyt Dr.
Newburyport, MA 01950
978-465-8950

Kenzer & Company
25667 Hillview Ct.
Mundelein, IL 60060
847-540-0029

Khalsa Brain Games
1390 Waller St.
San Francisco, CA 94117
415-626-5215

Koplow Games Inc.
369 Congress St.
Boston, MA 02210
617-482-4011

150

Kosmos Verlag
PO Box 10 60 11
Stuttgart
70049 Germany
+49-711-21910

Lance & Laser Models Inc.
211 E Northwood Ave.
Columbus, OH 43201
614-291-3703

Lightning Print Inc.
1136 Heil-Quaker Blvd.
La Vergen, TN 37086
615-287-5815

Limestone Publishing
11511 80th St. NE
Albertville, MN 55301
763-497-9998

Lone Wolf Development
42058 John Muir Dr.
Coarsegold, CA 93614
559-658-6980

Looney Laboratories
5003 Geronimo St.
College Park, MD 20740
301-441-1019

Mattel
333 Continental Blvd.
El Segundo, CA 90245
310-252-2000

Mayfair Games Inc.
8060 St. Louis Ave.
Skokie, IL 60076
813-707-6659

Milton Bradley Div. of
Hasbro
443 Shaker Rd.
East Longmeadow, MA
01028
413-525-6411

MoonDragon Trading
Company
6820 N 42nd St.
Milwaukee, WI 52309
414-540-9876

Multi-Man Publishing
403 Headquarters Dr. Ste. 7
Millersville, MD 21108
912-882-5174

Musashi Enterprises Inc.
2613 S 30th St.
Milwaukee, WI 53215
414-383-7791

New Deal Playing Card Co.
917 Illinois Street
Lawrence, KS 66044
785-331-4424

Non Sequitur Productions
1513 N. 69th Street
Wauwatosa, WI 53213
414-840-8115

O'Brien Publishing Inc.
10391 S. Shepard Ave.
Oak Creek, WI 53154
414-768-0168

Off World Designs
317 Huntington Way
Bolingbrook, IL 60440-2112
630-739-5274

Omega Games
PO Box 2191
Valrico, FL 33594
813-661-3804

Out Of The Box Publishing
LLC
PO Box 14317
Madison, WI 53714
608-244-2468

Pagan Publishing
5536 25th Ave. NE
Seattle, WA 98105
206-528-7665

Palladium Books
12455 Universal Dr.
Taylor, MI 48180
313-946-2900

Patch Products, Inc.
PO Box 268
Beloit, WI 53512-0268
800-524-4263
patch@patchproducts.com

Patterson Printing
Company
1550 Territorial Rd.
Benton Harbor, MI
49022

PBM Graphics Inc.
415 Westcliff Rd.
Greensboro, NC 27409-
9786
336-664-5800

Pegasus Publishing
PO Box 1845
Sherman, TX
75091-4999
903-893-4999

Phage Press
PO Box 519
Detroit, MI 48231
313-533-3122

Pinnacle
Entertainment
Group Inc.
PO Box 10908
Blackburg, VA
24062-0908
540-951-3749

Placebo Press
PO Box 16192
Lansing, MI 48901
517-267-0793

Precedence Entertainment
PO Box 28397
Tempe, AZ 85281
480-894-1812

151

Pressman Toy
Corporation
200 Fifth Ave. Ste. 1052
New York, NY 10020
212-675-7910

Pro Edge
PO Box 888
Vernon, NJ 07462
201-764-1120

ProFantasy
Software Ltd.
18-20 Bromell's Rd.
Clapham Common
London SW4 0BG UK
44 0 171 738 8877

Pulsar Games
12839 Patrick Ct.
Fishers, IN 46038
317-841-8992

R Talsorian Games
16212 NE 57th St.
Redmond, WA 98052
425-869-2649

R&R Games Inc.
PO Box 130195
Tampa, FL 33681-0195
813-835-0163

Ravensberger
Spielverlag
Postbox 1860
Ravensberg
88188 Germany
+49-0 751-86 0

Reaper Miniatures
PO Box 293175
Lewisville, TX 75029
972-434-3088

Reveal Entertainment
Inc.
3701 W Lake Rd.
Abilene, TX 79601-2701
915-677-8550

Rio Grande Games
PO Box 45715
Rio Rancho, NM 87174
505-771-8813

Robert Yaquinto
Printing Co Inc.
4809 S. Westmoreland
Dallas, TX 75237-1619
214-330-7761

S F R Inc.
100 N. McCormick
Oklahoma City, OK 73127
405-376-5819

Sabertooth Games Inc.
610 Industry Dr.
Tukwila, WA 98188
206-574-0238

Sanguine Productions Ltd.
2692 Madison Rd 1-PBM-279
Cincinnati, OH 45208-1320
312-803-1961

Score Corporation
1517 W N Carrier Pkwy
St. 155
Grand Prairie, TX 75050
817-983-0162

Skeleton Key Games
300 Lenora St. #270
Seattle, WA 98121
206-256-6303

Slave Labor Graphics
848 The Alameda
San Jose, CA 95126-3119
408-971-8929

Sovereign Press Inc.
PO Box 517
Williams Bay, WI 53191
262-245-6235

Sparticus Publishing LLC
3406 Grace Ellen Dr.
Columbia, MO 65202
573-474-4510

Specialty Graphic
3531 Sitro Bath
Carlsbad, NM 92009
760-635-5956

Steve Jackson Games Inc.
PO Box 18957
Austin, TX 78760
512-447-7866

Stupendous Games
2804 E. Oakland
Bloomington, IL 61704-4587
309-662-4208

Talicor Inc.
14175 Telephone Ave. Ste A
Chino, CA 91710
909-517-0076

Talon Games
PO Box 849
El Dorado, KS 67042
316-320-1599

Team Frog Studio
4908 Valley Ridge Dr. #3027
Irving, TX 75062
214-497-9580

Thunderbolt Mountain Mini
Inc.
656 E. McMillan
Cincinnati, OH 45206
513-861-8849

Topps Company Inc.
One Whitehall Street
New York, NY 10004-2109
212-376-0300 #114

Torchlight Games
207 14th St. #1F
Hoboken, NJ 07030
201-963-7005

Troll Lord Games
5620 Evergreen
Little Rock, AR 72205
501-663-2897

Troy Laminating & Coating
421 S Union St.
Troy, OH 45373
937-335-5611

Tundra Sales Organization
415 1/2 Division St. S Ste 1
Northfield, MN 55057
507-645-2708

U.S. Games Systems Inc.
179 Ludlow St.
Stamford, CT 06902
203-353-8400

U.S. Playing Card Company
4590 Beech St.
Cincinnati, OH 45212
513-396-5700

Universal Games Inc.
PO Box 2280
Atascadero, CA 93423-2280

University Games
2030 Harrison St.
San Francisco, CA 94110
415-503-1600

The Upper Deck
Company LLC
5909 Sea Otter Pl.
Carlsbad, CA 92008
760-929-3412

USAopoly
565 Westlake St.
Encinitas, CA 92024
760-634-5910

Valiant Enterprises Ltd.
PO Box 204
Antioch, IL 60002
847-395-3636

Victory Graphics
1210 Lincoln Ave.
Ottawa, IL 61350-4433
815-434-1929

White Wolf Publishing Inc.
735 Park N Blvd Ste 128
Clarkston, GA 30021
404-292-1819 (x264)

Winning Moves Inc.
100 Conifer Hill Dr. STE 102
Danvers, MA 01923
508-777-7464

Wizard's Attic
900 Murmansk St. Ste 7
Oakland, CA 94607
510-452-4951

Wizards of the Coast
PO Box 707
Renton, WA 98057-0707
425-204-8008

WizKids Games LLC
15821 NE 8th St. #100
Bellevue, WA 98008
425-641-2801

Z-Man Games Inc.
PO Box 98
Eastchester, NY 10709
914-793-1970

153

Distributors

AAAces
855 Inca St.
Denver, CO 80204
303-595-0237

Aarmstrong MCP
Hobby Distributors
6580 Vine Ct., #A
Denver, CO 80229
303-287-9185

ABC Northwest, Inc.
3130 22nd St. SE
Salem, OR 97302
503-364-2107
www.abcnw.com

ACD Distribution
2825 Index Rd.
Suite C
Madison, WI 53713
877-836-6910

Aladdin Distributors
1420 Cliffe Rd.
Burnsville, MN 55337
952-890-8700

Alliance Game
Distributors, LLC
1101 Greenwood Rd.
Baltimore, MD 21208
800-NOW-GAME

Alliance G. D. LLC/
Midwest
3405 Centennial Dr.
Fort Wayne, IN 46808
800-444-3552

Alliance G. D. LLC/
Southwest
9204 Brown Ln.
Suite 160
Austin, TX 78754
800-424-3773

Alliance G. D.
LLC/West
7544 W. Sunnyview
Visalia, CA 93291
888-366-5456

Alliance G. D. LLC/
Michigan
25090 Terra Industrial
Dr.
Chesterfield Twp, MI
48051
800-895-1145

Alliance G. D. LLC/
Berkeley
2950 San Pablo Ave.
Berkeley, CA 94702
800-424-4263

Alliance G. D. LLC/
Torrence
2012 Abalone Rd.
Torrance, CA 90501
310-618-0766

Berkley Publishing
Group
200 Madison Ave.
14th Floor
New York, NY 10016
800-223-0510

Black Hawk Hobby
Dist.
14255 Hansberry Rd.
Rockton, IL 61072
800-747-GAME

RJ Boyle Ltd.
32518 Dequindre Rd.
Warren, MI 48092
888-775-3730

Brookhurst Hobbies
12188 Brookhurst St.
Garden Grove, CA
92840
714-636-3580

Centurion Hobby
Distributors
92 North Main St.
Windsor, NJ 08561
609-918-0005

Checkmate
International
PO Box 621624
Littleton, CO 80162
800-747-1088

Diamond Comic
Distributors
1966 Greenspring Drive
Suite 300
Timonium, MD 21096
800-45-COMIC
www.diamond
comics.com

Excelsior Entertainment
Clifton Ind. Ctr.
100 Mill St. #20
Clifton Hts., PA 19018
610-622-3161

FM International
913 Stewart St.
Madison, WI 53713
608-271-7922

Gameboard Distributors
PO Box 721
Snellville, GA 30078
800-914-2597
www.gameboard.com

Georgia Music -
Home Office
4300D Highlands
Parkway
Smyrna, GA 30082
888-333-9500

Georgia Music - Florida
317 S. Northlake Blvd
Suite 1008
Altamonte Springs, FL
32701
888-767-5411

Hobbies Hawaii
Distributors
4420 Lawehana St. #3
Honolulu, HI 96818
808-423-0265

Hobbies Unlimited
73 Snake Hill Rd.
North Scituate, RI 02857
401-934-1824

Jones & Masters
395 Tennent Rd.
Morganville, NJ 07751
908-536-2040

Mad Al Distributors
2507 Fairbanks St.
Anchorage, AK 99503
907-274-4115

Motorbook International
729 Prospect Ave.
Osceola, WI 54020
800-458-0454

New Century
Distributors
1733 H St. Suite 330
PMB# 537
Blaine, WA 98230
604-596-4320

Osseum Entertainment
PO Box 1326
Maple Valley, WA 98038
425-271-5308
www.osseum.com

RPV Distributors
580 W. Lambert St.,
Suite K
Brea, CA 92821
714-671-1270

Sports Images
2G Gill St.
Woburn, MA 01801
781-938-4340

Trost Modelcraft &
Hobbies
3129 West 47th St.
Chicago, IL 60632
800-367-8624

Wizard's Attic
900 Murmansk St.
Suite 7
Oakland, CA 94607
510-452-4952
www.wizards-attic.com

Wright One
Enterprises, Inc.
909 Southeast
Everett Mall
Way, Suite B-200
Everett, WA 98208
425-355-5005

154

Brokers

While this is by no means a comprehensive list of legitimate brokers, every company on this list has a proven record of selling products to the largest publishers.

Jonathan Becker
Anjar Company
200 Fifth Avenue, Suite 1305
New York, NY 10010
212-255-4720
www.anjar.com

George Delaney
Delaney Product Development
6956 Hawthorne Lane
Hanover Park, IL 60103
630-837-2952

Andrew Berton or Adam Wolff
Excel Development Group
1123 Mount Curve Ave.
Minneapolis, MN 55403-1128
612-374-3233
www.exceld.com

Frank Young or Liz Farley
Franklin Associates
6381 Maple Rd.
Mound, MN 55364
952-495-1016
www.franklinassoc.com

Paul Lapidus
TTG/New Funtiers
9882 Cow Creek Drive
Palo Cedro, CA 96073
800-846-0701
www.newfuntiers.com

Gary Carlin
Inventor's Greenhouse
198 Tremont St. #505
Boston, MA 02116
617-422-0922

Michael or Lynn Marra
Marra Design Associates
7007 Dakota Ave.
Chanhassen, MN 55317
952-937-8141
www.marradesign.com

Peter Carr
Cactus Marketing Services
1553 S. Military Hwy.
Chesapeake, VA 23320
888-215-7040
www.cactusmarketing.com

Michael Molinoff
Electronic Licensing
Organization, Inc.
386 Park Avenue
South, Suite 1900
New York, NY 10016
212-328-2288

Frederick Fierst
Fierst and Pucci
64 Gothic St.
Northampton, MA 01060
413-584-8067

Jeff Hibert
Hibert Interactive
625 13th St.
Manhattan Beach, CA 90266
310-796-0207

Mike Trunfio
Invention Incubator
69 Graymore Rd.
Waltham, MA 02451
781-373-1776

Shelly Goldberg
Lot O Fun Marketing
17257 Quesan Place
Encino, CA 91316-3935
818-788-9087

Carol Rehtmeyer or
Eric Sakumoto
Rehtmeyer Design
& Licensing
1952 McDowell Rd., Suite 207
Naperville, IL 60563
630-717-9304
www.toyngames.com

Dan Lauer
Haystack Toys Inc.
8631 Delmar Boulevard,
 Suite 300
St. Louis, MO 63124
314-983-0985
www.haystacktoys.com

Richard Blank or
Howard Jay Fleischer
How Rich Unlimited, LLC
16 West 23rd St. 4th Floor
New York, NY 10010
212-366-6862
www.howrich.com

Bob Fuhrer
Nextoy
200 5th Avenue, Suite 1011
New York, NY 10010
212-243-1050
www.nextoy.com

Mark Cochrane
The Games Agency
Ground Floor, 21 Elmdale Rd.
Clifton, Bristol
BS8 1SH, UK
44 117 974 4711

Iain Kidney or Philip Harland
Games Talk
Little Coster, Blunsdon Hill
Blunsdon, Swindon
Wiltshire, SN2 4BZ, UK
44 179 370 5291

Jacqui Lyons
Marjacq Micro
34, Devonshire Place
London W1N 1PE, UK
44 171 935 9499

David Kremer or
Christine Trussell
Seven Towns Ltd.
7 Lambton Place
London W11 2SH, UK
44 171 727 5666

155

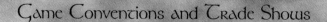

Game Conventions And Trade Shows

Conventions are consumer events where game-lovers gather to play, swap, and buy games. Trade shows are professional events where manufacturers show their new products to distributors and retailers, make deals, and otherwise schmooze. There are dozens and dozens of game conventions throughout the year. This list covers only the few most important ones.

Toy Fair

When & Where: February, New York City, New York
Description: The American International Toy Fair is the largest toy and game trade show in North America, with over 2,000 manufacturers, distributors, importers, and sales agents from 30 countries. Toy Fair is where the biggest manufacturers and retailers get together to make deals. It's the most important show of the year for mass market games. You need a professional connection to the industry to attend this show. Most inventors rely on brokers or agents to attend for them.
For More Info: http://www.toy-tia.org/AITF/index.html

GAMA

When & Where: March, Las Vegas, Nevada
Description: Sponsored by the Game Manufacturers Association, the GAMA Trade Show is an industry-only event where North American manufacturers, distributors, and retailers gather to check out new products, discuss release plans for the coming year, and pitch their distribution services. The 2001 GAMA Trade Show hosted over 300 stores, 250 product lines, and 57 distributors. You need a professional connection to the industry to attend this show.
For More Info: http://www.gama.org

The GAMA organization is also a critical resource for information on manufacturers and retailers. Their Web site is recommended reading.

GAMA
P.O. Box 1210
Scottsdale, AZ 85252
480-675-0205

Origins

When & Where: July, Columbus, Ohio
Description: Origins is America's second-largest game convention, with attendance of over 10,000 people. Emphasis is on hobby gaming and specialty games. Origins runs a prestigious awards ceremony called the Origins Awards where industry professionals honor each year's most critically acclaimed games.
For More Info: http://www.originsgames.com

Gen Con

When & Where: August, Indianapolis, Indiana
Description: Gen Con is North America's largest gaming convention, with attendance somewhere above 30,000 people. It's mostly focused on hobby games, but has a fair contingent of the European and American specialty markets as well. It's the best place you can go if you want to meet people in the industry. The show's focus is on gaming 'till you drop. Gen Con is owned and operated by Wizards of the Coast founder and former CEO Peter Adkison.
For More Info: 800-529-EXPO (3976)
http://www.gencon.com

TGIF

When & Where: September, Las Vegas, Nevada
Description: The Toy and Game Inventors Forum is different from other trade shows in that its primary purpose is for professionals involved in development of toy, game, and entertainment products to help each other. Its attendees are inventors, entrepreneurs, and publishers who come to network and discuss the industry. Carol Rehtmeyer of Rehtmeyer Design & Licensing runs the show.
For More Info:
http://www.toysngames.com/tgif/register.htm

Essen Spiel

When & Where: October, Essen, Germany
Description: Attracting more than 140,000 visitors, hundreds of journalists, and over 500 exhibitors from 17 countries, Essen Spiel is the biggest consumer game convention in the world. Unlike American shows, the

Warhammer 40K Space Ork

focus is more on checking out new products than playing old favorites and there's a broad mix of consumer types. All markets are well represented here, with the emphasis obviously on European games.
For More Info: http://www.merz-verlag.com/e/spiel/

Industry Publications

Comics & Games Retailer

A guide for hobby shop retailers to share information on topics like sales trends, promotional tips, and new products.
700 E. State St.
Iola, WI 54990
715-445-2214
www.comicsretailer.com

Playthings

The premier magazine for professionals in the broader toy and game industry.
360 Park Avenue South
New York, NY 10010
646-746-6400

Scrye

A hobby game magazine focused mainly on collectable games like *Magic: the Gathering*, *Mage Knight*, and the *Pokémon Trading Card Game*.
700 E. State St.
Iola, WI 54990
715-445-2214
www.scryemag.com

InQuest

A somewhat broader hobby game magazine covering trading card games, collectables, and roleplaying games, with a sophomoric sensibility.
Wizard Entertainment
PO Box 656
Yorktown Heights, NY 10598
203-266-7110

Dragon

The premier magazine for the roleplaying games industry, offering insight and game play material for *D&D* and d20 system games.
3245 146th PL SE, Suite 110
Bellevue, WA 98007
Phone: 425-289-0060
Fax: 425-289-0073

158

Dungeon

A monthly collection of *D&D* adventures. One of the best places for aspiring roleplaying game authors to get a foot in the door.
3245 146th PL SE, Suite 110
Bellevue, WA 98007
Phone: 425-289-0060
Fax: 425-289 0073

White Dwarf

Games Workshop's monthly magazine. Covers only Games Workshop miniatures products.
6721 Baymeadow Dr.
Glen Burnie, MD 21060-6401
800-492-8820

Games Magazine

A monthly magazine focused mainly on brain teasers and puzzles, but with good coverage of new games. A nice place to read reviews and get your game reviewed.
PO Box 184
Fort Washington, PA 19034
800-426-3768

Games Quarterly

A catalog of manufacturers and all the games they produce, focused on hobby and specialty games.
80 Garden Center
Broomfield, CO 80020
303-469-3277

Game Trade Magazine

Game Trade is a hobby and specialty game magazine put out by Alliance Game Distributors to promote the products they carry. An easy way to get a look at most of the important products in these markets.
1966 Greenspring Dr., Suite 300
Timonium, MD 21093
410-560-7100
www.gametrademagazine.com

Sample Query Letter

Q: What is a query letter?

A: You use a query letter to introduce yourself to a company you've never worked with before. It's also a good way to find out whether or not the publisher is interested in seeing a game like yours in the first place. You should never send an actual game prototype to a company that hasn't asked for it. A query letter sends a message that you're both professional and have done some amount of homework, factors that can also influence a publisher's reaction to future submissions. Query letters work fine over both e-mail and regular mail. When you address the letter, it really helps if you can get the name of the person who reads submissions. Sometimes this can be as simple as calling the company receptionist and asking, "Who looks at new submissions?"

160

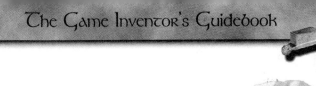

June 30, 1999

John Doe
Super Cool Games Company
1234 Fifty-Sixth Avenue
Los Angeles, CA 54321

Dear Mr. Doe,

I'm writing to ask if you would be interested in evaluating my new board game titled "Mutant Monkeys From Mars." I notice your company publishes a number of adult board games, but you don't have a science-fiction game. Looking at the other science-fiction board games on the market, I believe my game is both easier to learn and more fun to play, with a surprising twist.

In "Mutant Monkeys From Mars" players assume the roles of Martian monkeys who break out of the zoo and drink too much radioactive beer. Players roll dice and draw cards to see which beers they drink first. As players move their wooden monkey tokens across the board, they try to collect cardboard mutation tokens. The one with the most mutations at the end is the winner. The hook is that the game comes with an audio CD that lets players actually hear the sounds of drunken Martian monkeys while they play!

The game is aimed at 18 to 25 year-old college students, who have been my main playtesters. I'm a college student and lifelong game fan, so I have a good understanding of their needs. After playing it, one fraternity group even asked where they could buy it. I think the game has great potential and could be an exciting addition to your product line.

If you are interested in reviewing the game, please contact me at:

Your Name
P.O. Box 1294
Renton, WA 98057
999-555-1212
youre-mail@address.com

Sincerely,

Your Name

Sample Record of Disclosure

Q: What is a record of disclosure?

A: In the past, game companies have frequently been the target of frivolous lawsuits alleging that the companies stole ideas from an inventor. Although there are extremely few verified cases of a company actually stealing an idea, these lawsuits are still costly to defend against. To prevent this kind of litigation, many companies require every inventor to sign a record of disclosure statement, which essentially says the publisher can do whatever they want with your idea without giving you a cent. Upon reading the statement, it may seem like you're helping them take advantage of you. I recommend signing it anyway. I believe successful companies virtually never steal ideas. If a company ever did, it would be shunned by future inventors— stealing ideas is a business strategy that just doesn't make sense. A game is infinitely more likely to die because its inventor is overprotective than it is to be stolen. So my advice is to read documents like this carefully, but keep in mind that you are usually exposing yourself to very little risk if you decide to sign it.

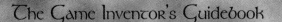

RECORD OF DISCLOSURE AGREEMENT FOR GAME SUBMISSION

The undersigned (hereafter called "APPLICANT") hereby agrees to the following:

APPLICANT submits the attached game, written material, or other idea ("GAME") voluntarily and on a confidential basis.

APPLICANT acknowledges that this GAME and its review by the reviewing company (hereafter called "PUBLISHER") does not establish any relationship between PUBLISHER and APPLICANT not expressed herein.

APPLICANT agrees that PUBLISHER may accept or reject this GAME and shall not be obligated to APPLICANT in any way until PUBLISHER enters into a written agreement with APPLICANT, and then only according to all of the terms of said agreement.

APPLICANT also declares that the GAME is original and is the APPLICANT'S own work and contains unique, novel, and/or public-domain material. APPLICANT declares that he or she possesses all rights necessary to enable PUBLISHER to use the GAME without any permission from any other party.

APPLICANT understands that the GAME may be similar or identical to ideas that PUBLISHER has independently designed or that has or may be brought to PUBLISHER from other sources. APPLICANT agrees he or she shall not be entitled to any compensation by reason of the use by PUBLISHER of such similar or identical material.

APPLICANT shall retain a copy of all materials submitted to PUBLISHER and hereby releases PUBLISHER from liability for loss of said materials. PUBLISHER shall have no obligation to return to APPLICANT any of these materials.

This Agreement shall be governed by the laws of the State of [Insert State]. Any disputes arising out of or relating to this agreement or any breach thereof will be settled by arbitration in accordance with the Rules of the American Arbitration Association.

Agreed and Accepted By:

APPLICANT
By:
Print Name:
Address:
Date:

PUBLISHER.
By:
Print Name:
Title:
Address:
Date:

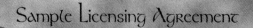

Sample Licensing Agreement

Q: What is a licensing agreement?

A: A licensing agreement is what you sign to give a game company the right to publish your game. Typically it spells out exactly what the game company can do with it, where they can publish it, how long they can publish it, and most importantly, how much money you receive.

GAME LICENSING AGREEMENT

This Licensing Agreement is made between PUBLISHER, [Insert Address] and INVENTOR, [Insert Address].

Whereas, INVENTOR has created the concept, rules, and materials for the board game called GAME.

Whereas, PUBLISHER wishes to obtain an exclusive worldwide license from INVENTOR to manufacture, market, and sell GAME anywhere in the world.

Whereas, INVENTOR declares that the GAME is original and is the INVENTOR'S own work and contains unique, novel, and/or public-domain material. INVENTOR declares that he or she possesses all rights necessary to enable PUBLISHER to use the GAME without any permission from any other party.

Be it known, in consideration of these premises and the mutual promises set forth below, the parties hereby agree as follows:

INVENTOR hereby grants to PUBLISHER an exclusive worldwide license to market and sell the GAME under the terms and conditions of this agreement.

Unless terminated under this agreement, the license will begin at the date of this agreement and shall continue for a term of three years. After the initial three-year term, the license will be renewed automatically, year to year, except that this Agreement may be cancelled by either PUBLISHER or INVENTOR, at any time by giving six months notice in writing to the other, in which case PUBLISHER will have the right to sell any stock remaining in inventory, subject to the royalty provisions of this Agreement.

PUBLISHER agrees to pay INVENTOR royalties consisting of 6% of the wholesale price to a retail or distribution customer for all games sold in the United States. It is understood that this price may vary from customer to customer.

If the game is sub-licensed to a foreign company for production then the royalty received from that company for sales in the foreign company will be split, with INVENTOR receiving 50% and PUBLISHER receiving 50%.
The amount of the royalty shall be calculated twice annually for goods produced during the previous six months. Royalties will be paid to INVENTOR no later than sixty days after the last of each six-month period. With each royalty payment PUBLISHER will furnish INVENTOR with a statement setting forth in reasonable detail the manner of calculation of royalties payable under this Agreement with respect to each royalty period.

Except as set forth in this Agreement PUBLISHER agrees not to use the artwork, images, or likenesses comprising GAME for any use whatsoever without the written consent of INVENTOR.

PUBLISHER agrees to use its best efforts at all times to promote and sell the GAME so as to provide maximum returns to itself and INVENTOR.

The parties agree that the relationship of PUBLISHER and INVENTOR is that of licensor and licensee, and that nothing in this agreement shall create a partnership or joint venture or establish INVENTOR as an employee or agent of PUBLISHER.
This Agreement and any amendments may be executed in counterparts, all of which will constitute one and the same Agreement. This Agreement may not be amended or modified except by an amendment in writing signed by both parties. This Agreement shall be binding upon, enforceable by, and shall inure to the benefit of the successors and assigns hereto, except that PUBLISHER shall not assign, sublet, or otherwise transfer its right under this Agreement to any third party without the express written consent of INVENTOR.

If any provision of this Agreement should violate any law it will not affect the validity of the remainder of this Agreement.
To protect the exclusivity granted to PUBLISHER by this Agreement, INVENTOR will take all necessary steps to prevent the sale of the game within the territory except as the same may have been produced within the terms of this Agreement.

Agreed and Accepted By:

APPLICANT
By:
Print Name:
Address:
Date:

PUBLISHER.
By:
Print Name:

Title:

Address:

Date:

Sample Option Agreement

Q: What is an Option Agreement?

A: You sign an option agreement when a company isn't sure whether or not it wants to publish your game but wants a long time to think about it. Normally companies only take six to eight weeks to consider a new product submission, but if they decide they need more time they sign an agreement like this. It essentially says that they have a specified amount of time (such as a year) to decide whether or not to publish it. In the meantime, you can't offer it to any other company. In return, they pay you cash, called an option fee. When the time is up, the company has either decided to publish the game or returned it and you may submit it to another publisher.

166

OPTION AGREEMENT

The undersigned (hereafter called "APPLICANT") and reviewing company (hereafter called "PUBLISHER") hereby agree to the following:

APPLICANT grants to PUBLISHER the exclusive right and option to purchase from APPLICANT the publication licensing rights to the original board game, entitled "Mutant Monkeys From Mars" (herein called "GAME") developed by APPLICANT.

PUBLISHER is granted a 12-month exclusive option (herein "OPTION") to purchase all publication licensing rights to the GAME. The consideration for the OPTION is one thousand dollars ($1,000) and is due upon execution of this agreement.

PUBLISHER may extend the OPTION for an additional 6 months upon payment of an additional five hundred dollars ($500).

Upon exercise of the OPTION, PUBLISHER will pay a licensing fee equal to 8% of the gross wholesale sales.

APPLICANT agrees that he or she has the right to enter into this agreement and to grant all rights stipulated herein. APPLICANT also declares that the GAME is original and is the APPLICANT"S own work and contains unique, novel, and/or public-domain material. APPLICANT declares that he or she possesses all rights necessary to enable PUBLISHER to use the GAME without any permission from any other party.

This agreement shall be governed by the laws of the State of [Insert State]. Any disputes arising out of or relating to this agreement or any breach thereof will be settled by arbitration in accordance with the Rules of the American Arbitration Association.

Agreed and Accepted By:

APPLICANT
By:
Print Name:
Address:
Date:

PUBLISHER.
By:
Print Name:
Title:
Address:
Date: